KEN
DOHERTY

KEN DOHERTY

LIFE IN THE FRAME
MY STORY

KEN DOHERTY WITH DAVID HENDON

JOHN BLAKE

Published by John Blake Publishing Ltd,
3 Bramber Court, 2 Bramber Road,
London W14 9PB, England

www.johnblakepublishing.co.uk

www.facebook.com/Johnblakepub facebook
twitter.com/johnblakepub twitter

First published in hardback in 2011

ISBN: 978-1-84358-504-6

British Library Cataloguing-in-Publication Data:

A catalogue record for this book is available from the British Library.

Design by www.envydesign.co.uk

Printed and bound by CPI Group (UK) Ltd, Croydon, CR0 4YY

1 3 5 7 9 10 8 6 4 2

Papers used by John Blake Publishing are natural,
recyclable products made from wood grown in sustainable forests.
The manufacturing processes conform to the environmental
regulations of the country of origin.

Every attempt has been made to contact the relevant
copyright-holders, but some were unobtainable. We would be
grateful if the appropriate people could contact us.

For my mother and late father, for the start you gave me and the many sacrifices you made. For Sarah, for all your love and support. For Seamus, Anthony, Rosemarie and all my family, you have been my rock. And for Christian, you are the centre of my world.

CONTENTS

CHAPTER ONE

WORLD CHAMPION

Crucible Theatre, Sheffield, 5 May 1997

To be at the table on the final night of the World Snooker Championship, potting the balls you need to become the winner of our sport's greatest prize, is every player's dream.

It had been mine since I was a boy. I'd got into snooker through watching the weekly series *Pot Black* on television but I realised I wanted to be a professional – wanted to be world champion – when I saw Alex Higgins win his second world title in 1982. I was 12 years old and sat there transfixed. Alex was the most exciting player in the game and had helped to put it on the map through his brilliant play and well-documented off-table antics. I can still see him that night, stood on the stage at the Crucible Theatre in Sheffield after beating Ray Reardon in the final, tears rolling down his face, calling for his wife and baby daughter to join him as he cradled the silver trophy. It was such an incredible, unforgettable moment and I knew as I watched from my front room in Ranelagh, Dublin that I wanted to be part of that world. And there I was, 15 years later, about to follow in Alex's footsteps.

The odds were stacked against me going into the final. Stephen Hendry was unbeatable at the time. He'd won six world titles, including every single one since 1992. He had established himself as one of the greatest players in the history of the sport and the Crucible was like his back room. For these reasons, most people would have backed him to win but I believed in myself. It was, after all, only a two-horse race. I'd beaten him before and I saw this as my big chance to join the pantheon of snooker legends. I pictured myself lifting the trophy up in that iconic arena, the famous twinkle lights providing the backdrop for a hundred photographs as I held the silverware aloft. I imagined the applause and the acclaim. I had to believe I was capable of experiencing that because if I'd allowed myself to think about Stephen, about how good he was and the damage he could do, then I don't think I'd have won.

I went into the final full of hope with the feeling that I could come out on top if I played a good tactical match and punished his mistakes. I wasn't going to out-score Stephen or out-pot him, but I could compete in the safety department and I knew if he missed that I could feed off the crumbs. I got stronger and stronger as the match went on.

I'd led Stephen 15-7 before he won the last two frames of the third session. 15-9 was still a good lead but then he won the first three of the final session and suddenly it was 15-12. Like everyone else in the game, I'd seen him make incredible comebacks before, as when he'd come from 14-8 down to beat Jimmy White 18-14 in the 1992 final, so the pressure was on me. In the 28th frame, I made a break of 61 but he had a chance to steal it. That would have turned the match and made it an unpleasant 15-minute interval for me, spent contemplating defeat having held such a massive lead. However, he missed a red down a cushion and instead of 15-13 it was 16-12. I won the next frame and I was so relieved at that point that I felt great, as if I couldn't lose.

Potting the last few balls was just surreal. It was like it was happening in slow motion. I looked over to the press seats and saw Tony Drago, a Maltese player and a good pal of mine, with a big smile on his face and that started me smiling. I looked up to my friends in the crowd. I thought of Alex Higgins and my dad, who watched Alex's 1982 victory with me and who died when I was 13. I just wished he could have been there to see me do it.

Stephen shook my hand and then I was interviewed by David Vine of the BBC before the trophy presentation. I held up the cup just as I'd imagined, only the reality was far better. It was a fantastic feeling.

My family didn't come over for the final. They couldn't take the nerves and the pressure. A crew from RTE went round to my mam's house to film them watching the match but she'd gone out on her bike. She couldn't even take watching it on the TV. My two brothers, Seamus and Anthony, and my sister, Rosemarie, were there and they had press knocking on the door all day for interviews. They had the champagne on standby but were climbing the walls with nerves.

My mother ended up getting a puncture and had no way of knowing what had happened in the final. She didn't have a mobile phone and, anyway, she tried to avoid people in case they gave her the latest score. She just wanted to shut the final out until it was over. She had to walk back to the family home in Ranelagh from Donnybrook, pushing her bike all the way, and called in at a friend's house, which is how she found out I'd won.

My memory of winning the title was made more special by the way the Irish people celebrated with me and by discovering the impact it had had on so many of them. You don't realise when you're playing in a big match like that just how many people are living every emotion with you, willing on every pot and going through every little setback. I would discover just what it meant to everyone back home in the next couple of days.

After the final, I did press interviews and then went to the champion's reception at a hotel in Sheffield. We had a great party. Eamon Dunphy was there and quite a few other friends from Dublin, including the footballer Niall Quinn, who said he'd never experienced tension like it. We partied all night and I didn't get a wink of sleep. I rolled in at 9am and there was a press conference booked for 10. After that we went down to Ilford in Essex, where I'd been based for almost a decade. It was great to take the trophy down there so that everyone could get pictures with it.

I went home to Ireland on the Wednesday, two days after the final. We landed at a special place in the airport and I was told to let the passengers get off first and stay in the aircraft. Everyone was lined up on the runway: my family, press, airport staff, politicians. It was unbelievable. I came down the steps and my mother was first in line. I gave her a kiss and handed her the trophy.

I'd been in my own little world in Sheffield and didn't realise just how many people had been watching. I was told that the main police station in Dublin didn't receive a single call on the final night. Even the criminals had taken the evening off to watch me play Stephen.

I went on Joe Duffy's RTE show and he had George Best on one line, the boxer Steve Collins on another, footballer Paul McGrath on another and loads of other Irish sports stars who I looked up to and who'd been watching, wanting to congratulate me. It was then that I began to grasp how big a deal this was to Ireland and its people. I hadn't been aware of that when I was playing, which is just as well because all the excitement would probably have got to me and I wouldn't have been able to pot a ball.

We had a press conference at the airport and they laid on two buses that went through to the city centre, with me on one holding up the trophy. There were thousands of people lining O'Connell Street. Passing cars beeped their horns and people were leaning out of their office windows, waving and clapping. It was amazing. I felt like some sort of pop star. You see footage of football teams parading through towns and cities and everyone coming out to cheer them, but you don't think it will ever happen to a snooker player, least of all to you.

We stopped at the Mansion House on Dawson Street. They put on a reception inside and then we got back on the bus and went through to Ranelagh. We stopped again outside Jason's, the snooker club where I'd started playing, and had a party in there. Then we went to a couple of pubs, the Richard Crosbie Tavern and Russell's, where parties had been thrown for me. I had Gardai chaperoning me in case things got out of control, which I found strange to say the least. My life seemed to have changed within the space of a couple of days. I didn't want the guards but they insisted and they were friendly guys, so I sneaked out a Guinness or two for them.

The following weekend the people of Ranelagh threw a street party for me where they put up a bandstand. I got up to make a speech and said I was proud to be world champion, proud to be Irish, proud to be a Dubliner and proud to come from Ranelagh. My mother and I sang *Molly Malone* and everyone was coming up to me, offering their congratulations, and I could see how genuinely happy they were that this kid they'd known for years had become world snooker champion. It seemed everyone wanted to shake my hand and touch the trophy. I celebrated with old friends from school and complete strangers alike.

Those sorts of scenes could never have been repeated. Even if I'd won it again, it wouldn't have been as special so I drank it all in. I knew it was something to savour. When people close to you follow your sporting career they have to go through all the disappointments as well as the highs. They feel your pain so it's wonderful when they can also share in your joy. They'd always believed in me and supported me, even when I hadn't been doing so well.

I'd had a bad run leading up to the World Championship. Steve Davis hammered me in the Masters at Wembley and also in my home event, the Irish Masters, and then I lost in the first round of the British Open. Ian Doyle, my manager, lambasted me in the newspapers, saying I was lazy and not making enough of an effort to improve my form. Ian was the sort of guy who would use the press like that to motivate his players but what he said shook me up. I felt I'd been doing all the right things but I think his comments focused my mind and made me more determined. I wanted to prove him wrong and show everyone, and most especially myself, that I was capable of being a world class player.

In 17 days at Sheffield I'd gone from feeling low and struggling for form to beating the best player in the world in the biggest tournament of the year. Outside of having children and getting married, there's no feeling like picking up that trophy. I just wanted to give it a big kiss and hold it up in the air. Nothing as a player will ever beat that moment. The hairs on the back of my neck still stand up when I watch other players win the World Championship and lift up the trophy, as it brings my own personal memories of that special night flooding back.

No matter how many other tournaments you win or other great moments you experience, nothing tops winning the world title. You'd swap all the other tournament wins for one at the Crucible. Your name will always be on the trophy and people will always come up to you with a story of where they were watching or what they were doing when you won it. You're etched into the history of the sport and to be part of that is very special. That's why the reaction from the public was so positive, because they recognised what a big deal it was.

I really appreciated the reception I received from the people of Ireland and enjoyed every minute of all the celebrations, but it was also nice to finally come home and just be with my family. I promised my mother that if I ever won the trophy she could keep it on top of the television set and that's what she did for the next year. She hadn't wanted me to become a snooker player. She'd felt it was too risky a profession and had wanted me to follow the academic route instead. It was hard for her. She went through all of the emotions with me. I didn't really understand the extent of that back then but I've begun to now that I've become a parent myself.

The trophy rarely left the TV set. People would come round just to have their picture taken with it. I paraded it at Old Trafford, Croke Park and Lansdowne Road but it belonged in my mother's front room. Every day she gave it a kiss and she kept getting it shined up so that it sparkled. I would often come in and have a look at it to check my name was actually on it with all the other great champions.

And it was. It had really happened. I'd really done it: the high point of a career that's been quite a ride.

CHAPTER TWO

THE LOWEST DEPTHS

Prestatyn, 5 August 2009

I'm sitting in Pontins holiday camp in North Wales. The sun is shining and the place is full of holidaymakers enjoying a summer break on the windswept coast. Kids are having fun on the karting track and gangs of lads are playing football on the sliver of grass that separates the chalets.

Why am I here? Well, not by choice. I've had such a poor run of results these past two years that I am no longer ranked high enough to receive an automatic place at the main venues. I have to pre-qualify and that means coming to Prestatyn, where most of the qualifiers are staged. I've just played Rod Lawler in the third qualifying round of the Shanghai Masters in one of eight small cubicles used for these early rounds of tournaments, which most people never witness. There were seats for around 20 spectators but it was by no means packed. To get back to the players' room from the arena you pass Captain Croc's Adventureland, which is full of young children being entertained by, among others, a seven-foot tall furry creature by the name of Zena the Hyena. The Crucible it isn't.

It's a humbling experience. A man came up to me earlier, all friendly, and said, 'How are you doing, Ken? Do you still play?' I can forgive the question. I only played twice on television last year and failed to qualify for all but one of the ranking tournaments. I had dropped out of the elite top 16 – the group who are seeded through to all the venues – in 2008 but last season was an even bigger disaster. I fell to 44th in the official rankings, which is worked out over two years. On the provisional list, which is just last season's points, I'm 55th. If I fall below 64th by the end of the campaign next May I will be off the tour. I've come here in full knowledge that I am now fighting for my professional survival.

Prestatyn holds happy memories for me, or rather it did until last year. I first came here as a teenager in 1988 for the huge spring festival, which featured something like 1,000 players. I just wanted to give it a go and see how I would get on. I loved it. The snooker boom was still in full swing and the camp was crawling with people of all ages, every one of them with a cue in their hand, getting stuck into what was in every sense a festival. Wherever you looked there were matches going on and the craic was fantastic. It didn't have the serious edge that inevitably comes with proper professional tournaments. I got through to the last 32 and played Mike Hallett, who at the time was one of the best players in the world. I was in my torn jeans, T-shirt and trainers and he came in wearing his pristine suit, freshly ironed shirt, patent shoes and dicky bow, looking a million dollars. He gave me 21 points start per frame and I beat him and went on to win the tournament. I'd brought £500 with me, thinking this would last me a long time. That's how naive I was. For winning the title I picked up £2,500 and it set me up for my amateur career.

So I had been looking forward to coming back to Prestatyn because it's where it all started for me, but the one thing I was fearful about was the difference in atmosphere between the big arenas that I was used to and the cramped cubicles the qualifiers are played in. You get accustomed to the TV cameras and the crowd and that gets the adrenalin flowing but here there's hardly anyone watching and it all feels flat, as if you're not involved in a professional event at all. I think any player – even Ronnie O'Sullivan or Stephen Hendry – would struggle if they had to come back to playing in this sort of set-up after all those years in the limelight. You don't realise just how spoilt you've been until it's all taken away from you. Coming here feels like starting all over again.

I was slightly in denial about it all last season. I thought, 'Well, I only have to win one match in each tournament to qualify' so if I could just get off to a good start then I'd be OK. I told myself not to worry about it but as the first match approached I found myself becoming nervous. The nerves grew and grew and I hardly slept the night before because I was full of trepidation. I was playing Jimmy White and, as much as I like him, I didn't want to play him because he'd already won three matches and was in good form, plus he had vast amounts of experience and wouldn't be overawed playing me, like some of the younger players might have been. It felt like all the pressure was on me. My hands were shaking and I couldn't settle down. I could barely hold the cue.

As I sat watching Jimmy take advantage of all my mistakes I was thinking, 'How has it come to this?' Two years previously, I was in the World Championship quarter-finals against Marco Fu. If I'd beaten him I would have been world no.1. As it was, I finished second in the rankings and yet here I was, mired in the qualifiers and unable to cope with the new environment. It had been such a sudden decline that I was completely unprepared and didn't know how to feel about it or get my head around how to stem the slide.

Jimmy beat me 5-1. In the next tournament I had to play another of the old guard, John Parrott, and he whitewashed me 5-0. Judd Trump, a talented teenager, handed out another 5-0 hammering in the next tournament and, to complete the misery, Jimmy beat me in the last event, also 5-0. So from my four matches in Prestatyn, the place where my career had lifted off two decades earlier, I won one frame.

After that last defeat, I went to catch the train to Holyhead to get the ferry back home. I sat on the platform and just wanted to cry. In fact, I very nearly did. I was all alone and felt like I was deep in a black hole that I couldn't see out of. I felt like throwing my cue in front of the train and possibly me along with it. I'd been world champion, I'd enjoyed success and acclaim in various parts of the world but right now I couldn't win a match. I could barely win a frame. I didn't know where my career was headed. I was 39 and I thought, 'Is it all over? Is that it? Is it going to end here like this?' I was thinking that I would drop off the tour and that would be it: I'd no longer be a professional snooker player. That's how low my confidence had sunk. It didn't matter what I'd done previously in my career. None of that seemed important now because my self-belief had gone and I had only dark thoughts. From enjoying such highs in the sport, I'd fallen to the lowest depths.

Things got worse when I failed to qualify for the Crucible. The qualifiers were actually played in Sheffield at the English Institute of Sport a few miles from the game's theatre of dreams, but Gerard Greene beat me and that meant I wouldn't be part of the World Championship for the first time in 16 years. It was horrible to know our sport's biggest event was taking place and that I wasn't in it. I love watching the game but it's so hard when you're not involved. I did go to Sheffield for the last five days to work for the BBC, which was great fun but it isn't the same as playing. Nothing beats playing.

At that point I gave myself one more season. I knew I couldn't bear much more than that because it was beginning to depress me and detract from the great store of memories I've amassed in my years in snooker. I didn't want all that to be soured by me being unable to produce performances I could be proud of. I didn't want to be in the position where I was just turning up at tournaments to make up the numbers. I'd rather not play at all than be in that position.

The season ends when the World Championship ends. When I got home after John Higgins's victory over Shaun Murphy I had a long think about where I was going and told myself that I had to keep fighting. The only way to turn things round would be to put the work in, put the hours in on the practice table. The alternative was to feel sorry for myself, lie down and accept that my career was over. I just couldn't do that.

I've never given in at any point in all my years in snooker so I decided to draw a line under that season. I had some alterations made to my cue, which gave me a new impetus, and tried to come into this campaign with a positive frame of mind. I made a conscious decision to play in everything that I possibly could, including small pro-ams, to get some match practice. I went to Sheffield to play at the World Snooker Academy, which is a great facility where the likes of Peter Ebdon and Ding Junhui practise. I needed to toughen myself and my game up. It's been hard because I have a young son, and I've hated being away from him, but I needed to make the effort to rescue my career.

Slowly, my confidence has started to come back through winning matches in these events and today I beat Rod Lawler 5-2, my first win in a ranking tournament in eight months. The relief is overwhelming. I feel like I've won a title.

I came here determined just to play and not think about the fact that I'm at Prestatyn or where I am in the rankings. I had such a bad year that I now have to play two qualifying matches in each tournament, but you have to just accept that and get on with it. Despite that, I was nervous as hell for the match with Rod. My stomach was churning over all the way through. I pinched the first frame on the black by clearing up from the last red and I did the same another three times in the match with good clearances. It's an awesome feeling when you win like that because I know I could easily have lost 5-2.

OK, it's one win in a cubicle in North Wales in front of maybe a dozen people. It's not a match that will live long in the memory or will be talked about in years to come. I haven't got a trophy out of it and there was nothing about it that would stand out for anyone else. But this win may – just may – be the confidence boost I need to turn things around.

CHAPTER THREE

GROWING UP

I've been lucky to have made good money playing snooker and I now live in a lovely house in Dublin with my wife, Sarah, and our young son, Christian. I can appreciate some of the material luxuries we have these days because I certainly didn't have them as a boy. Life was pretty tough for my parents.

I'm the third of four children. My brother, Seamus, is eight years older than me. Anthony is five years my senior and my sister, Rosemarie, is the youngest by two years. I was born on 17 September 1969 to my father Anthony and mother, Rosemarie. They both worked a multitude of mainly low-paid jobs to provide for us as children.

My first home was in Swan Place in Donnybrook. We lived in the back of a sweet shop owned by an elderly woman until she sold it to a young couple, Mr and Mrs O'Connor. They decided they could make a profit by selling it on but would first need to get rid of us, and so it was that they made our lives a living hell.

One of my earliest memories, when I was about three, was of the landlord coming in and kicking my toys all round the room. It was the first time anyone had been mean to me and it will always live with me. One Sunday we went out and by the time we returned they'd changed the locks so we couldn't get back into our own house. There was a window where the latch would fall if you kept on pressing it so we were able to climb through there, the only way we could enter. I have only vague memories of this but there is a photograph in the *Irish Times* of my mother holding me as she climbed through the window. That was the first time I ever appeared in a newspaper.

They kept on threatening us. One of them told my mother, referring to me, 'I hope your little bastard dies.' I don't understand how anyone could be that cruel, especially about a young child, but if their behaviour showed up the worst of humanity, my parents and the strength they showed in the face of such hostility emphasised the best. They refused to be bullied or let the constant intimidation prevent the family from living as normal a life as possible.

Eventually it went to court and they gave us compensation of £2,000 but you needed £3,500 to buy a house. We were given a deadline to leave but had nowhere to go so were facing an uncertain future. My dad's family home was owned by a guy called Mr Cook, who also owned a couple of properties in Ranelagh, a district of Dublin, and he heard that we were in trouble. Someone who lived in the top half of one of his houses had just died so he offered that to us. So we moved from a small dwelling to an even smaller one.

Our new house had three rooms between the six of us. There was a lounge room that was also a kitchen, so small that the stove was out on the landing, and there were two bedrooms. The toilet was outside and we had a bath out there once a week, one after the other. That might sound grim by today's standards but I remember being a happy child. I didn't know any different and had nothing to compare it to. Thanks to my mother there was always food on the table and we were always well clothed. My parents struggled all their lives for money. At one stage my mother had four jobs and also had to look after the four of us. I didn't know it then but when I look back I realise that they were hard times, but at least we were together as a family.

My mother was relentless in trying to find us a new house. She had left home at 18 to join Muckross Park convent and had made connections there. The daughters of various politicians went there and she lobbied anyone she knew after hearing that the Dublin Corporation were building four new houses. It was down to her that we got our new home, a much bigger one than the first two, complete with a letter from Charles Haughey, who would go on to become Irish prime minister. It read: 'Dear Mr and Mrs Doherty, I hope you will be happy in your new home.'

My mother would do anything for anyone. If someone was suffering she would be there to help. She used to make dinner for people who lived on their own, put it on a plate and get on her bike and take it round to them. She'd take people in who needed a bed for a few nights. She was tough, because she needed to be, but was also caring and couldn't bear to see anyone going through a bad time. She taught me to consider other people and to be grateful for what I had.

I looked up to Seamus, particularly after our father died because he had to assume that fatherly role. He was 21 when our dad died and had to become head of the household. He was the one who first took me to Jason's, where my boyhood enthusiasm for snooker blossomed into a lifelong passion. You would only be allowed in with an adult so if he hadn't taken me with him I might never have got the chance to play snooker regularly. He actually won the first snooker trophy ever brought back to our household. I'm still close to him now and ask him for advice and wisdom when I'm in a spot. He's very easy to talk to and always ready to help.

I never got on with Anthony at all when I was growing up. I used to fight with him all the time and was forever teasing him. I think he felt I was just constantly out to wind him up and in a way that's true. To me, it was just a bit of a laugh but he didn't always see it that way. In fact, when I'd go to the bus stop for school he wouldn't stand next to me. He pretended that he didn't know me, let alone that he was related to me. He'd even walk to the next bus stop rather than be seen with me. We'd be endlessly arguing and scrapping but when I got a little older we became close. We'd go out drinking together and have a really good time because Anthony is such great company. He's a little off the wall but very funny and all the old stuff from childhood is forgotten, or if we do talk about it then it's to have a good laugh.

I spent a fair amount of time with Rosemarie when I was a young kid because we were close in age but as we got older we developed our own interests and had separate circles of friends. For me it was sport and she wasn't that interested in all of that. She has a lovely family of her own now and we talk often on the phone. We were all raised as such a tight-knit unit that it's not surprising we should remain that way, even though we've all got houses and lives of our own. We live reasonably close to each other and know that if any of us needs help with something the others will come running.

I don't think I was a badly behaved child but I got into scrapes. One time, we went to the Isle of Man on holiday. I would have been seven years old. We were staying in a bed and breakfast and I shared a room with Seamus. One night he got up to go to the toilet, which was out on the landing, and I thought it would be funny to lock the bedroom door. That might have been a good joke except that I got back into bed and immediately fell asleep, so when Seamus returned he couldn't get back in. Being a considerate sort, even as a teenager, he didn't want to wake anyone else up so he gently knocked on the door and whispered for me to open it but I didn't hear him so he started banging on it. That still didn't wake me but it did wake the landlord and the other guests, who by now were all out on the landing, demanding to know what the commotion was all about. I think I may have eventually woken up but by then I was too scared to open the door.

On the same holiday, myself and Anthony spent a lot of time messing around, giving each other stick and doing things like kicking each other under the breakfast table. It got so bad that we'd have to sit at different tables – my father with Anthony and my mother with me. I had this ball and I kept throwing it at Anthony's head to wind him up. He was going down some stairs and I threw it at him, catching him full on the head. So he picked it up and came after me, throwing it in my direction. Then I threw it back at him, but instead of hitting my brother it caught a porcelain plate on the wall, which smashed into several pieces on the floor. It cost my mother £15. Bearing in mind the most she would have had to spend during the week would have been £50, it wasn't a very enjoyable holiday after that.

People often ask me how I got the scar on my face. It happened at a birthday party for Donal O'Sullivan, a neighbourhood friend of mine, when I was seven. He had a shed at the end of his garden and we'd sit on the roof and enjoy the sunshine. On this day we were messing around on the top of the shed as kids do. My cousin was spitting at my feet and I was walking backwards to avoid it into what I thought was the side of the house. I was expecting a brick wall to be there but I was faced round the wrong way and, in fact, there was nothing there at all except a solid drop.

All I remember is falling backwards and then later being brought round. I had fallen into an old tin bin full of bricks and junk and broken my arm in three places. I must have put the arm out to break the fall, which probably saved my life. If I'd gone in head first I would have been a goner. I caught my face on the jagged edge of the bin and that's how I cut it and eventually got the scar.

The father of the house picked me up and carried me down to my mother's. I'll never forget what happened when she opened the door and saw me there all bloodied. She screamed and screamed and my father laid me down on the couch. We didn't have a phone but one of the neighbours did and they rang for an ambulance. I don't remember everything that happened next because I was only semi-conscious. I know I was sent to hospital but they said I'd have to go on to the children's hospital and, as they didn't attend to the cut immediately, the scar formed. Looking back, I was lucky I wasn't more badly injured or even killed. It's certainly something I won't ever forget.

There were a few guys in Ranelagh who got in trouble with the police and they would show you how to shoplift from a local store. A few times I stole, helping myself to sweets and biscuits. It wasn't high-level crime but it was still wrong and I'd die if my own son ever got involved in something like that. Eventually my mother caught me with bags of sweets in my coat pocket and as she knew I couldn't have afforded them she set about dragging the truth out of me. Finally she got me to admit that I'd stolen them and then scolded me with a wooden spoon. She was disappointed in me because she had had to work so hard for everything that she had, which wasn't much, and everything she'd given us. It made me feel ashamed and I never did it again.

I was lucky that I had snooker. It was something to focus on and a way out of a life of trouble that I could quite easily have drifted into without anything to concentrate on or strive for. I was mad into football as well, playing as much as I could, but had to make a choice when I was 15 between the two sports because there were snooker tournaments on Saturdays and they were beginning to clash with football. I was captain of the Rathmines Boys side but I also wanted to play in the snooker events. I knew that if I was going to be serious about one of them then the other would have to go. And the great thing about snooker was that you didn't play in the rain, you didn't exhaust yourself and there were no hard tackles. I was also starting to earn money from winning snooker tournaments. Looking back, it was only pennies but it felt like riches to someone who had never had any money before. I'd turn up at school with a load of sweets that I'd bought, not stolen.

I went to the Westland Row Christian Brothers school and loved my time there. It's often stated that proficiency at snooker is the sign of a misspent youth but it wasn't true in my case. I worked hard and genuinely enjoyed it. Both my parents drilled into me the importance of doing my school work. My mother said she would let me play snooker as long as I got my homework done first. She said that if my grades started slipping she'd take my snooker cue away from me, which was the worst punishment I could imagine. And it worked because I did knuckle down and did all the work I had to. I never missed a day of school through illness or skiving off in my life, even though I knew I wanted to be a snooker player. Education is the cornerstone of your life. You never stop learning and I'm glad I did work hard, unlike a lot of the boys at school who had no interest in it at all.

I loved history, chemistry, French and Spanish. They were my best subjects and I did seven Highers, although I had to drop down in maths because it was just too difficult – I never have been any good at maths. I only got a C in the end but I passed the rest with honours. The teachers were good to me as I got older and my career developed, and would let me take time away if there was a big amateur tournament to play in. One of them, Paddy Finnegan, was doing a roll call once, going through the names, and he turned to me and said, 'Doherty, I notice you missed about 20 days last year playing snooker. I hope we'll see a bit more of you this year.' I replied, 'Well actually, sir, I'm off to New Zealand to play in the World Amateur Championship, so I won't be around for the next three weeks.'

I had a lot of mates in school. One of my best friends was a guy called Derek Davis, who suffered from epilepsy. We played football together for Rathmines and had been in school with each other right from our primary days. Sometimes I used to have to take him home after he'd had a fit, although he faked a few as well if he wanted to get out of a lesson. He died aged 28 – he'd been to a party and had a fit when he returned home. It was unbelievably sad.

The only thing I disliked about school was getting up early. I haven't become much keener on that as I've got older, but I knew I had to work hard because there was no guarantee back then that snooker would be a career for me. I was doing well as a junior but the professional game is a completely different proposition and I couldn't be sure I'd turn out to be a success. Even in the late 1980s and early 1990s the financial rewards lower down the ranking list were meagre. You had to be a top player to earn any sort of living and little has changed.

I learned my trade in Jason's, which was round the corner from where we lived. It wasn't just a club: it was a meeting place and a crucial part of the Ranelagh community. They had a jukebox in there that played hits of the 1970s and early 1980s and the kids would hang around it, putting on songs and messing around. There were also space invaders machines, pinball and table football. To me, it was like another world. It was full of life and adventure, noise and people. I was so excited that they'd let me in and went on to spend a huge amount of my adolescence in there.

At that time Jason's had mainly pool tables. There was one snooker table and rather than have a light above it, as is normal practice, it was next to a window, so the sunlight lit it up. That's how I started playing. I was so short I'd have to stand on a biscuit tin to reach the balls. I used to get off the 48A or the 44 bus from school. I'd pass by my house, go straight into Jason's, put my school bag and coat under the table and then I'd have to clean out the ashtrays and sweep the floor. After I'd done that Ambrose Collins, one of the guys that ran the club, would let me play a game of snooker with him, just one frame. Then I'd be allowed to play a few games of pool and space invaders. That's what I did every single day.

My first final was the Evening Herald Under 16s. I lost 2-1 but people were starting to see I had potential and that was mainly down to Jason's. I owe the lads there a great deal. I couldn't have improved as a player without their help and kindness. The club was run by two brothers, Derry and Jack

Cosgrave, and they did so much for me, giving me a chance. It was just an hour each afternoon but it brought me on considerably and kept my enthusiasm for snooker simmering. I kept a book of who I played and what the score was so that I could record my progress. I couldn't have afforded to play that often and may well have drifted away from snooker without the regular practice and the support I was getting.

I was coached by Paddy Miley, an international player who organised handicap tournaments. Paddy had great knowledge of the game and also the experience to know how to approach matches, especially when it came to the tactical side of snooker. He would teach me that you didn't need to go for everything, you didn't have to pot them all in one go. You could play safe, be patient and force mistakes from your opponent. It was a valuable lesson to learn and gave me a clear advantage as an amateur because I was playing guys who didn't have that insight into match-play snooker.

I played my first snooker against a professional at Jason's when I was 13. Eddie Charlton, the great Australian player of the 1970s and 1980s, came to do an exhibition and I played a frame against him. It was ironic because I would go on to play him in my first televised match eight years later.

The exhibition was at 11 o'clock on a Saturday morning. I used to play football on Saturdays so I came in with my gear in a bag, put a football under the table, played Eddie and then went off to soccer. I enjoyed playing Eddie and I gave him a good game before he beat me on the blue. He was a great character who was known for cursing under his breath. If you got a bit of luck against him you'd hear him mutter, 'You lucky bastard!'

Eddie was known for being hard as nails in a match situation but in the exhibition he was good value. He was very funny and did an impressive trick-shot routine, including shots I'd never seen up close before. I was disappointed because the lads from Jason's were going out for lunch with him afterwards but I had to go to football. I'd have loved to have heard some of the old stories because I'd watched Eddie on *Pot Black* and it was exciting to meet him.

In that small way it gave me a taste for the big time. When Eddie came into the club everyone knew who he was, because he was a well established player who you often saw on the TV. He'd won *Pot Black* and been runner-up in the World Championship three times. I suppose as a 13-year-old I looked at the regard he was held in and fancied a bit of that myself. Of course, I would have to work for it.

My mother wasn't so impressed with the time I was spending in Jason's. Many a time she'd come in brandishing a wooden spoon and threaten me with it if I didn't come home. She'd send my sister round to tell me my dinner was on the table and then if I didn't come home she'd come down herself and chase me out. When you're involved in a game, you don't want to stop and there were times when I'd try and hide from her in the club, although she'd always find me. One time she threatened Derry Cosgrave with her wooden spoon. She told him: 'If Ken fails his exams, I'm holding you responsible.' This to a grown man!

I don't think she believed snooker would ever be a career. She's always been a worrier and can't bear to watch me play. Even when I won the World Championship she had to go out because she got too nervous watching on the TV. She once came down to Goffs in County Kildare where they used to play the Irish Masters but spent the whole match out in the car park with her rosary beads. She wanted me to succeed but was worried for me in case it went wrong. She'd rather I got a proper job, one that wasn't so risky and uncertain.

But I knew snooker would be my life. My first century was 100 bang on when I was 15, which is late by today's standards, and my first title was the Irish Under-16 Championship. My mother still has the trophy in her kitchen to this day, alongside all my other trinkets.

My only sadness is that my father wasn't alive to witness my rise to the top of snooker. I was 13 when he died in June 1983. We'd not long moved into our new council house and were all excited by the change in circumstances. It felt like it was a new start for the family but my dad died just two years later.

I was in Jason's playing snooker and someone I used to play pool with came in and said, 'Your father's been taken to hospital.' I ran home and my brothers told me that Dad had had a heart attack outside a shop in Ranelagh. He suffered from angina and had a clot in his leg. He'd been waiting to go in for an operation but they didn't have a bed free. So he waited and waited and still there was no sign of the operation. It went on so long that my mother actually told him to go out and feign a heart attack, just so he would finally be treated, but he was too proud to do that.

Dad was taken to St Vincent's hospital on the Wednesday evening where he underwent emergency treatment. It was a horrible couple of days because we didn't know whether he'd pull through or not. We all went to the hospital but I was too scared to go in and see him, which is one of the few regrets I have in life. Nothing had prepared me for something like this and I didn't know how to cope with it. I was frightened beyond belief: the happy little bubble in which I lived my childhood had been shattered.

On the Friday afternoon we went back to the hospital but by the time we got there he had died. I remember just standing outside with Rosemarie, both of us bawling our eyes out through shock and disbelief. He was only 58. We were all devastated. My mother had to take Valium to get her through the next couple of weeks. She had lost the love of her life. After going through so much hardship, things had seemed to be turning round for Mum. She had the new house and four children but to lose her husband was a terrible blow. Typically, though, she was determined to do the right thing and she took to bringing us up on her own, using her inner strength and moral values. I don't think she could have done a better job. I've no doubt we were a handful at times but we had such love and respect for her that we stayed in line most of the time. She did everything for us, took us swimming or to tennis, for days out, for a picnic. We'd have a holiday every year at Butlin's and though we weren't well off, we didn't go without love.

All you can hope for in life is that your children turn out well, that they're happy, they're safe, they have a good job, a family and stay out of trouble. I only really understand this properly now that I'm a parent myself. I'm far more unselfish now that I have a son because all I'm concerned with is his well-being, and my mother was the same when we were young.

After my father died I felt that everything I did was for my family and he was the first person I thought about after winning the World Championship. He'd bought me a six-by-three-foot table for Christmas but never really saw me compete because I didn't become a serious player until after his death. The guys at Jason's saw how upset I was and could not have been more helpful. They gave me free practice at the club and then started sponsoring me to enter events. Eventually they gave me a brown envelope each week with twenty quid in it and I'd use the money to try and hustle and double it up. I'd come home late at night and rub the money in Mum's ear. I was determined to repay what she'd done for us.

My biggest challenge, though, was to persuade her that I should leave home and move to England to pursue a career as a professional – a big, daunting step for me and my family and not one my mother liked at all.

CHAPTER FOUR

ILFORD

By the time I was 18 I recognised that if I wanted to reach the level required to have a successful professional career then I would need to play better players more regularly. I had achieved what I could in Ireland, so I would have to move to the UK where there was a vibrant pro-am scene at the end of the 1980s. It made sense for another reason: all the main tournament qualifiers were held there.

The big step for me wasn't moving to England but telling my mother of my decision. She didn't want me to go. In fact she was horrified. She wanted the family to stay together and didn't believe snooker was a proper job, never mind a career I could earn good money at. I reasoned with her. I said I wanted to go over to give it my best shot. I didn't know if it would work out or not but I knew I would regret it forever if I didn't at least try to make a go of it. I said if it didn't work out I'd come back home. At the time I was on the dole, 35 quid a week, and it wasn't a lifestyle I enjoyed. I couldn't keep living like that and snooker was in my blood, so I tried to make her understand that it was my dream and it could be one of the most important steps I would ever take.

My mother cried her eyes out but the rest of the family were supportive and managed to talk her round. She knew deep down that I'd made my mind up because this was my great ambition in life and eventually she gave me her blessing, cautious though it was. I didn't blame her: she had fought so hard to keep the family together through the hard times and now one of her children was telling her he wanted to go and live in another country. But it wasn't a betrayal: I was trying to make good on the start she had given me in life and make something of myself. I didn't want to leave my family but it was a sacrifice I knew I had to make and I couldn't delay it any longer. Time was ticking on and it was a question of taking a leap into the unknown or staying in Ireland and standing still.

I chose Ilford in Essex because Eugene Hughes lived there. Eugene was a successful Irish player who reached no.17 in the world rankings and won the World Team Cup three years running with Alex Higgins and Dennis Taylor. I went over with a friend of mine, Anthony O'Connor, who was also trying to make it as a professional. I stayed with him at his auntie's house in Turnham Green, west London. We'd get the tube to Barking and then hop on the bus to Ilford Snooker Centre, where Eugene arranged free practice through the owner, Ron Shore. So we could play to our hearts' content. We couldn't have asked for anything more.

It was a fair way to travel each day but Eugene very kindly let us stay in his house nearer the club. He was a great personality, always full of fun with a similar sense of humour to us. We were on his wavelength and he kept our spirits up when we were feeling homesick. I learned a lot about snooker as well through playing Eugene. He was a very clever player with bags of experience behind him and he helped my game to develop. Without his support I may not have lasted in England, because despite having been so excited to go over, it was a huge wrench for me and I missed my family like crazy. Irish families are often very close and I phoned mine all the time. It was painfully difficult to be separated from them but at the same time it was a great adventure for me. I was standing on my own two feet and starting to experience the world outside Ranelagh.

Myself and Anthony were joined by Stephen Murphy, Damien McKiernan and Finbar Ruane, Irish snooker lads who came over to try their hands at the game, although Finbar had by then stopped playing and just fancied a change of scene. We shared accommodation for a couple of years and although there wasn't much money knocking around it was some of the best fun I've ever had. We stayed mainly in bed and breakfasts or rundown rented places. There was one B&B run by an Irish couple. We paid them £50 a week and they did our washing and gave us our meals, so it was like a home from home. The only problem was that she was mad and he was even madder.

There was one time when he tried to kill himself – and the rest of us as well. He'd had some argument with his wife and decided to end it all by turning on all the gas rings on the cooker in the kitchen. He went up to bed and waited for the house to blow. I was in the room next door to him and his wife but, luckily, Damien used to work for Ronnie O'Sullivan's dad in his sex shop in Soho and would come home late, at around three in the morning. When he came in through the front door that night he could smell the gas so he didn't turn the lights on. He went to the kitchen, turned off the gas and opened all the windows. If he hadn't, the whole house would have been blown apart and us with it.

For some reason we decided that we had to find somewhere else to live. We stayed one more night and this time the guy got completely drunk and had another argument with his wife. He was so drunk that he fell down on the landing, totally naked, while his wife was screaming, 'Help me! Help me!' By now we'd had enough. It was another in a long line of domestics and we didn't want to get involved because we didn't know what he was capable of, but we plucked up the courage to drag him to his bed and locked the door behind him. His wife was in bits crying, saying he'd been having an affair, that she'd walked past an estate agent and seen that the house was up on the market, that she'd come home and found him hanging from the banister and had had to cut him down, and that on New Year's Eve he'd filled the bathtub and tried to drown her in it. None of this made us feel like changing our minds about leaving. I'd lived there for three months and I had put myself in danger. If it hadn't been for Damien, I could have died under that roof.

We would get to Ilford Snooker Centre at ten in the morning and leave at ten at night. We basically lived at the club. We'd have all our meals there – pie, chips and beans; scampi, chips and beans; roast chicken, chips and beans; fish and chips. Chips came pretty much as standard. We were at the age when people go to university and that's similar to how it was for us, only we were playing snooker. We were living cheaply, eating cheaply and drinking cheaply. I didn't go out as much as some of the other boys at the weekends because there was always a pro-am to play in and some good money to be won. The standard of opposition was high. Some more Irish guys came over to play, including Stephen O'Connor and Joe Swail, and Ronnie O'Sullivan's dad would send a taxi for me to go to his house and play his boy, who would have been 12 or 13 at the time.

Stephen Murphy and myself joined King's Cross Snooker Centre's league team with Frank Maskell and a lad called Peter Ebdon, who would go on to become world champion. To be honest, we only joined the team because they were guaranteeing us free snooker and free steak and chips. It was £3,000 for the winners and we did win the league title but never saw the money. There was some dispute because we weren't members of the King's Cross club and we never got a penny.

The weekends would be focused on pro-ams, mainly the ones in the south of England, although we did sometimes venture up north to places like Leicester and Manchester. It was a learning experience. Coming up against different players gave you a different perspective of how the game was played. I'd been brought up to play quite a cautious game, making 30 or 40 and then putting colours safe, leaving the cue ball on the back cushion. I'd learned the game against older guys who had that experience but the pro-ams were full of players my age and they all had their own approach, their own way of playing.

I could never play like Alex Higgins but I loved his attacking style. However, people forget what a brilliant safety player he was as well. He had a great snooker brain and you could learn a lot about the tactical side of the game from watching him, although people don't tend to remember that so much. It's true I always erred on the side of caution because when I was learning my trade I had twenty quid in my pocket and I was playing for double or nothing, so I wasn't going to go in with all guns blazing. I had to be careful otherwise I'd lose the lot. But I've made more than 200 century breaks as a professional and there's only a dozen or so players who have done that, so it would be wrong to call me a grinder. If the balls are there I will pot them and I found that the open snooker being played in a lot of these pro-ams suited me.

I decided to stay in Ilford after I joined the circuit and started achieving some success. I bought my own flat there in the end, which we'd been renting for a year. It was a good place to be based, because Essex was a strong snooker area and there were always high quality opponents to practise with. It's important to keep your game sharp between tournaments and in any case I liked the environment and most of the people. There was always a buzz in the club. Plus, it was close to London and easy to get back home to Ireland from there.

I remained in Ilford until I won the World Championship in 1997. I'd been going out with a girl in Ireland and she moved over to Essex in early 1996 but I discovered she'd been messing around with one of the Ilford guys while I was away at tournaments. It completely did my head in because I saw it as a betrayal, not just by her but by the people at the club. I thought I had friends there but some of them were laughing at me behind my back. I took the trophy to the club, mainly to thank Ron Shore for all he'd done for me, and then went back home. I was in a terrible state. I felt let down and humiliated. I'd been in love with this girl but she'd cheated on me with one of my mates and the Ilford crowd were telling other guys on the circuit about it. It broke my heart and affected my confidence, but when I won the World Championship it felt like sticking two fingers up to the lot of them. I'd achieved my dream and nobody was going to sour it.

Ilford Snooker Centre has closed down now, which makes me sad because it was a great place full of characters and competitive snooker. Many clubs in the UK and Ireland have also shut down – Jason's did in 2005 – for a number of reasons. Interest in snooker has declined from the enormous levels it reached during the boom years of the 1980s, which were always going to be impossible to sustain, plus the smoking ban has seen many members drift away from them. A lot of people don't realise that snooker clubs are not just about snooker. They are also social hubs where people congregate for a drink and a smoke, a chat and a bit of banter, an evening out of the house. That's now been lost from many areas, which is a shame but perhaps a reflection of the way society has changed.

Snooker clubs are like families and a place to meet and chew the fat. When they close down, as with Jason's, everyone goes their own way and you miss the craic and the laughter. You miss the mix of people and the community aspect of everyone having a gathering point. It's gone now from Ranelagh and from Ilford too. I'm just glad I had both at the time when I needed them.

When I left Ilford I came back to Jason's and installed a Riley table I'd been given for winning the World Championship. They built me a match room and put pictures on the wall celebrating moments from my career. I had enough money to buy a three-bedroom house and it was like I'd never been away. I was back in Ranelagh and it felt like nothing had changed.

Nobody treated me any differently. I was welcomed back with open arms and a lot of the old characters were still there, like Scobie Murphy, who brushed and ironed the tables and couldn't bear to eat anything hot. His diet was basically ice cream. He once got a sausage from the fish and chip shop and put it in a puddle in the street to cool it down. I hadn't realised how much I'd missed the likes of Scobie until I moved back home. They always treated me as just one of the lads in Jason's, before I moved to Ilford and when I came back to Dublin as world champion. The one difference was that I no longer had to clean out the ashtrays and sweep the floors.

But moving to Ilford had definitely been the right decision for me. I think even my mother recognises that now. It not only helped my snooker but assisted my development as a person and made me more independent and worldly wise. In many ways it was a gamble but it paid off, although when I first moved there I had still to get on the professional tour, and that proved to be a frustratingly difficult process.

CHAPTER FIVE

BACK IN THE GAME

Shanghai, 11 September 2009

It's hard to explain just how fantastic it feels to be at a snooker venue as a player rather than a TV pundit, which was pretty much the only reason I came to tournaments last season. I've just lost 5-0 to Shaun Murphy in the quarter-finals of the Shanghai Masters. You might think that would be a huge disappointment, and I guess on one level it is, but Shaun is the world no.3 and a former world champion, he played superbly all through the match and it was my first ranking-event quarter-final in two and a half years. All things considered, I'm just happy to be here.

The day after my win over Rod Lawler at Prestatyn I beat my pal Fergal O'Brien 5-4 to qualify for the final stages. I knew that match wouldn't be easy but I found that, having beaten Rod, I was more relaxed. I was able to go for shots that I might have backed away from before and I held myself together really well in the deciding frame. I rediscovered some of that fighting spirit that had been lacking when my confidence had begun to evaporate last season.

Having booked my place on the flight to China I won the second Pro Challenge Series event of the season. This is a new series of small events designed to give the players some additional playing opportunities and extra cash. The tournament I won was played using just six reds instead of the traditional 15 and, although it wasn't on TV and wasn't a big event, I was really chuffed to win. I'd made a concerted effort to play in as many events as I could and felt it was starting to pay off. Like most players, if I enter a tournament – big or small – I want to win it, so to come home with the trophy was another timely boost of confidence.

Because I was so far down the rankings, when I qualified for Shanghai I had to play a wildcard before my first-round match. I was drawn against Aditya Mehta, an Indian who was on the tour last season, and I beat him 5-0. Next up was Neil Robertson, ranked ninth in the world and a terrific long potter from Australia. I'd been commentating on him at the Crucible when he reached the World Championship semi-finals a few months earlier. In a way it was a weird feeling playing someone like him because I'd got used to the cubicles where I was up against lower-ranked players, but all of a sudden I was back in the big time with that buzz you get at major tournaments. Don't get me wrong – it was brilliant to experience that again but it took some readjusting.

I beat Neil 5-4 and then I beat Barry Hawkins, also 5-4. They were two good, battling wins. I think I proved something, to myself and everyone else in the game, because I'm well aware that the other players would look at me and think, 'Ken's gone. He's an easy draw now.' That's what I'd be thinking if I was looking from the outside in. I'd love to play someone like me who looks like he's lost the plot and is apparently finished as a top player. I hope I showed them I'd got the bit back between my teeth. I've always been renowned as being a fierce competitor and I think I've reminded a few people that I can still compete.

Sport isn't really a place for sympathy. Nor should it be. We all want to win and there's very little mercy shown. It's like being a wounded animal: you're lying there bleeding and the hyenas circle, ready to come in for the kill and finish you off. You can sense that as a player but when you have a bit of confidence, when it comes back, your body language changes and everyone else can see it too. They can see that you fancy the job now. When people fear you, when you can sense that they fear you, it gives you such a psychological boost and it helps you to play better.

I've won five matches in the first tournament of the season compared with just two in the eight events last year, so the other players will be aware that I've turned some sort of corner. It's up to me to keep it going but I feel completely different now to how I was on that train platform, tears welling in my eyes, thinking it was all over. It's amazing what a bit of confidence does.

When you're at the top and you're winning, you kind of

take it all for granted, as if it's easy, but anyone who has ever picked up a cue, whatever standard they are, knows that the game is very difficult and I appreciate it more now after the couple of years I've had. I'll never be complacent again. When you miss out on tournaments and have to watch them at home or from the commentary box it's embarrassing. You feel you should be out there, not the guys you are watching, and you miss it like crazy.

Can I get back in the top 16? I believe I can. It's going to be really tough but it's definitely possible. This run in Shanghai has seen me rise 18 places to 37th in the latest list, so it shows what you can do with a few results. One thing is for sure: I'm looking forward to the rest of the season, whereas last year I couldn't wait for it to end.

CHAPTER SIX

FROM AMATEUR TO PROFESSIONAL

In order to turn professional in the late 1980s you had to come through the Pro Ticket Series. These were a number of tournaments that had their own ranking list from which the top 24 contested play-offs to get on the main tour. I went into them full of confidence. I'd been doing well in pro-am events, felt happy about my game and was building a good reputation so I fancied my chances of turning pro in time for the 1989/90 season, as did my supporters.

But it all went wrong. I got to the quarter-finals of the play-offs but lost 5-1 to Dave Harold, who is still a very difficult player to beat, and that was my dream crushed, or so it felt. I would have to wait a whole year to try again while players like my friend Stephen Murphy had made it on to the tour. For them it was the most exciting time of their lives, for me a huge disappointment. Maybe I'd got carried away with my own reputation, or what I thought my reputation was.

Pat Caulfield, my mate who travelled with me, said that there was another way on to the circuit, by winning the World Amateur Championship. To get into that I'd have to win the Irish amateur title and that felt like a huge step backwards. I'd left Ireland to go and live in Ilford, so I considered it an embarrassment to go back, my tail between my legs, like I'd failed.

I was very down about losing to Dave Harold. I'd been so excited about the prospect of turning pro and it hadn't worked out. But I knew I still loved snooker and wanted to make a go of it. I had to snap myself out of the sulk I was in. When Pat first suggested playing in the Irish Championship as a way of getting into the world amateurs I turned round to him and said, 'Fuck the Irish Championship.' That's the frame of mind I was in but it wasn't the right attitude. So I went back to Ireland, entered the amateur championship and won it, beating Anthony O'Connor in the final. That meant I could go to Singapore for the World Amateur Championship but I was to make a foray to another foreign location before that.

When I was at the Isle of Wight playing in the Pro Ticket Series, a guy came up and introduced himself. His name was Curly Mick (obviously a nickname) and he explained that he'd seen me playing and wondered if I'd be interested in entering the World Under-21 Championship, which was due to be held in Reykjavik, Iceland. I said I hadn't heard of the event and in any case I couldn't afford to go. I'd earned £2,500 at Prestatyn for winning the Pontins Open but I wanted to hang on to a bit of money to tide me over. He offered to pay for my flight and hotel so of course I jumped at the chance to go.

I ended up winning the title, beating Jason Ferguson 9-3 in the final. The whole event was an adventure. I'd barely been anywhere outside Ireland and the UK before, so it was an eye-opener. It also exposed me to what could come my way in terms of attention if I did join the pro ranks. The matches were shown on Icelandic TV so when we went out to a bar we'd be recognised, which wasn't something I'd anticipated. I was signing autographs and felt like a star. It was great fun.

There was a player in the tournament called Ollie King, who was a good-looking lad and so got quite a bit of attention. He was in the toilets in one nightclub having a pee and some fans rushed in after him to get his autograph, so he was urinating with one hand and signing his name with the other.

I'd never had any sort of attention before and I realised that snooker was a sport that could give you a certain profile and earn you admirers. It made me even more determined to turn professional and be a part of that world. I wasn't interested in fame for the sake of it but to be admired for your profession, for your skill, was something that appealed, just as I'd admired footballers and guys in snooker like Alex Higgins.

I went to Singapore for the World Amateur Championship full of confidence having already won the world junior title. I shared a room with Anthony O'Connor and beat him in the last 16 before making it to the final, where I defeated Jonathan Birch 11-2. He didn't take the defeat too well. In fact he cried his eyes out. He'd been tipped for great things as England's next great amateur star who could possibly rise to the top of the professional game but I hammered him and he didn't like it. Well, why would he?

Singapore is a country I might never have visited but for snooker. I made some great friends there and experienced a different culture, which I always enjoy. But the trip was also an important one for my career. It made me realise that losing to Dave Harold was a blessing in disguise because it enabled me to play in the world junior and world amateur championships, and winning the two of them was a real boost of confidence. It also gave me more stature in the snooker world. I was the best amateur player on the planet and so the guys in the professional ranks would have to sit up and take notice of me when my time came.

I'm still the only player in the game's history to have won the world junior, world amateur and world professional titles, which is a proud achievement. I'm amazed that it's a record that has stood for over two decades. But back in 1989 I had no idea that Crucible glory awaited me. I just wanted to be part of the professional scene and my amateur victory meant that this was now going to happen.

Having won the world amateur title, I was invited to play the former world champion Fred Davis in a play-off in July 1990. If I won that I'd be on the professional circuit. It was exciting because this was my dream. I was confident because Fred, though one of the legendary names in the sport, was in his late seventies by this time and I would be a heavy favourite. As it turned out, Fred decided to retire, so I didn't have to play him and turned pro automatically.

My professional career began in September 1990 at the

Norbreck Castle Hotel in Blackpool. This was the year before the game went open so there were still only 128 players on the circuit. I didn't care how many there were – I was just excited to be taking these first steps. There was a wave of anticipation following me because I was world amateur champion and people were looking to see how I'd do. It was hard not to get caught up in that and I maybe put myself under a bit of pressure by listening to people making predictions and building me up.

I got off to a terrible start. I lost my first qualifying match 5-2 to a player called Jason Smith. A couple of days later I lost another qualifier, 5-1 to Dave Gilbert. It was a real baptism of fire. I'd had that arrogance of youth and assumed I'd just go in there and roll these guys over but they were seasoned campaigners who played hard match snooker, keeping you out with effective safety, and I wasn't ready for that. I hadn't done my homework and felt like I'd walked into a brick wall. It was gruesome. I learned a lesson because I'd fallen into the trap of believing the hype. I wasn't giving my opponents the respect they deserved and it backfired on me.

In the end, I qualified for two events, the Mercantile Classic and European Open, and then later in the season I reached the Crucible, all of which helped me to rise to 51st in the rankings after my first season.

Looking back, I was very naive in my expectations of what life would be like on the professional circuit. I thought it would all be red carpets, cameramen everywhere and glamour. Instead, it was freezing cold Blackpool in wintry October with hardly anyone watching as you slugged it out in the qualifiers in small, soulless cubicles.

I'd been hitching lifts to pro-ams for a while with Mark King and his dad, Bill, who would start coming to tournaments with me even if Mark wasn't playing. Bill drove me from Ilford to Blackpool in those early days, and he was a real character and great company. He was a bit of a ducker and diver, an Arthur Daley type who sold stuff out of the back of his Volvo, like tracksuits, alcohol and cigarettes. Bill became a father figure for me and he knew about the game so as well as looking after me, we could talk snooker. He was good to have around – apart from when we shared rooms. He snored so much he was like a big grizzly bear. But he would always have tales to tell about his army days in Egypt and kept my spirits up, helping prepare me for games and keeping my confidence high.

With Bill on board I didn't have to worry about getting to tournaments. I'd just hop in the car and he'd get me there. It took some of the early pressure off and allowed me to concentrate on my snooker. Because he was older, he was a calming influence and ensured I didn't go off the rails. Had I gone around with someone of my own age they'd probably have wanted to be checking out bars and chasing after women. Some of the guys in Ilford were like that but not Bill. I liked doing those things but realised I had to wait until after tournaments and not do it before or especially during a competition. Bill kept me on the straight and narrow in that respect.

I've seen so many good players, even when I was a kid starting off, with bags of potential who just wasted it. They didn't put in the hours practising because they wanted to be out partying. Some of them thought they'd made it before they actually had. Even when they turned professional they thought they'd arrived, not realising that in fact they had to work harder than ever to keep improving. There is always something to strive for in sport. Even if you reach the very top and become world champion, you still have to work hard to stay there. That's what the likes of Steve Davis and Stephen Hendry did. They were not only fantastic snooker players but had an unshakeable desire to remain at the top and keep winning titles. When they won a tournament they put it to the back of their minds and got on with the next one. It's a great shame to think that so many talented young players have pissed away their opportunities by drinking, messing about and not giving the game the respect it deserves. Sport is about hard work and you truly only get out what you put in. The worst thing in life is to look back and think about what could have been. As a young player I could recognise that and knew I didn't want to fall into that category. Having made sacrifices to come over to the UK I wanted to give my pro career my best possible shot.

My first TV match was against Eddie Charlton at the Mercantile Classic in Bournemouth. It was fitting because Eddie had been the first professional I'd ever played, when I was a kid. I beat him 5-2 but it was a weird experience playing in an arena with the bright TV lights and the cameras moving around. I couldn't believe how much they moved when you were on a shot. It was off-putting because I wasn't used to it and it's the same for the young lads today who experience that for the first time. But it wasn't overawing. I enjoyed it and wanted to keep coming back for more. Jimmy White beat me in the quarter-finals but I knew I'd be back. Although it took some adjusting to playing in the TV arena, I felt I would be comfortable there. I preferred it to the Blackpool cubicles.

To reach the Crucible I had to win five matches, although my first opponent withdrew. In the final qualifying round I beat Cliff Wilson 10-5 to get through to play Steve Davis, who beat me 10-8. After a slow start to the season my performances had seen me rise to 51st in the rankings. It wasn't the best campaign considering all the things I'd been tipped to do as world amateur champion but at least I had recovered from those early defeats and given myself something to build on.

My second season, in 1991/92, was more successful. I won the qualifying event for the Masters, which got me through to Wembley for the first time. I reached two ranking tournament semi-finals and the Irish Masters final, and although I missed out on the Crucible when Peter Francisco beat me in the qualifiers, I rose to 21st in the rankings, with a great chance to break into the top 16. Players today don't seem to make that sort of breakthrough as quickly but I think that's because of the way standards have risen. There was more dead wood around when I turned pro but the guys in the qualifiers are much tougher now.

Going up the rankings is all very well but you don't really arrive in any sport until you've won something. My first ranking title came in my third season when I captured the 1993 Welsh Open. It remains a very special moment in my career. I still have the draw sheet on the wall where I practise and it's weird looking at some of the names on it, most of whom no longer play on the tour.

The Welsh was my first success but it could have been the Grand Prix at the Hexagon Theatre in Reading, one of the established events screened on the BBC. In 1992 I beat Willie Thorne, Steve Davis and Terry Griffiths to play one of my idols, Jimmy White, in the final. I lost 10-9 but it was a cracking match. As you can imagine, the atmosphere was electric and I more than held my own. I made a huge break to force the decider but never got a really good chance to win it. Even though I ultimately missed out, I loved the experience of playing in the final. I felt that this was where I belonged – in the big time. I don't remember being nervous, or at least not so nervous that I couldn't hold my cue. I competed well but just came up short in the end.

However, it was only three months or so until I put things right in Newport. I started off my Welsh Open campaign by scraping past Steve James 5-4, then beat Gary Wilkinson 5-3 and had two good wins, over John Parrott and James Wattana, to reach the final. There I was up against Alan McManus. Alan was one of the best players of the time and very tough to beat. We had a right old scrap but I managed to beat him 9-7 and picked up a cheque for £27,000. I know that isn't a fortune compared with the bigger tournaments but it was the most I'd ever won and to get my hands on a trophy was a lovely feeling, just the best you can have as a sportsman.

I was only 23 and didn't have a big entourage with me. It was just me, Pat Caulfield and Bill King. We went to the post-final reception and then had a drink in the hotel. I don't think the final was broadcast in Ireland but they were still proud as punch when I took the trophy home the next day. So many people had talked about me as a potential tournament winner but until you actually do it there's always that bit of doubt whether you're really up to it. Even then there weren't loads and loads of tournaments and each one was very difficult to win. It was a tough era with Stephen Hendry as top dog, Steve Davis still playing very well, the likes of Parrott and White, McManus, Wattana and some of the old guard like Terry Griffiths, Dennis Taylor and Alex Higgins still hanging on. To win a tournament from that sort of field was an achievement to be proud of. It was a new era for snooker because it had just gone open. Anyone could now be a professional if they paid a membership fee and entry fees, so the circuit expanded from 128 players to around 700. Hendry had taken Davis's mantle and revolutionised the game in terms of the way it was played. Then you had Ronnie O'Sullivan, John Higgins and Mark Williams, who were all teenagers at the time, breaking through.

Those early days on the professional circuit were great times. I had come over to the UK with just £500 in my pocket, thinking it would last me a long time. Suddenly I was earning big money at a time when snooker was still second only to football on television. I'd been offered a management contract by IMG when I turned professional. They would guarantee me £25,000 per year regardless of what I earned on the table, but I ended up making a lot more than that. It was an insurance policy and it meant I didn't have anything to worry about, which was a great help because I could focus on playing. I've always been pretty level-headed and although the money excited me, it didn't go to my head as it has done to some other players. I didn't go out and buy a flash car. My first motor was a Ford Escort Eclipse. The first thing I wanted to buy was my own place, so I bought an apartment in Dublin.

I'd had a Halifax account, which I'd opened with the £500 I'd brought over with me. After a couple of years there was something like £60,000 in it. I couldn't believe it was actually mine and kept looking at the statements to check it was right. I didn't even have a credit card, just a bank book, and I'd take out money when I needed it. If I was tempted to go mad and start splashing the cash around, then I'm happy to say that I resisted. I can understand why other players do go a little crazy because most are working-class lads who have never really had much money and the snooker authorities don't give us any advice about what to do when we start earning large amounts. We're not advised about making investments or anything like that – we have to figure it out for ourselves. I think this is why so many players have been ripped off by so-called managers over the years, because they have more money than they know what to do with and put their trust in people who want to exploit them. Fortunately, I'd always been good with money and knew that just because I might earn £200,000 one year, it didn't mean I'd earn the same amount the following year.

After three years with IMG I signed for CueMasters – later 110sport – which was then run by Ian Doyle and subsequently by his son, Lee. They appealed to me because they knew the game inside out. They were already looking after Stephen

Hendry and several other players and they were good at finding sponsors and making you money off the table.

I built up a good relationship with Ian Doyle and John Carroll, who ran things for the company on the circuit, from the start and have been with the company ever since. Even when contracts were up I didn't have to sign a new one. It was taken for granted that I would stay with them and that suited me because it meant there wasn't too much legal stuff or formality. Ian would always say that whenever I wanted to leave I could and that he wouldn't hold me to any contract. We trusted each other and, even more importantly, we liked each other.

Stephen Hendry was the no.1 for Ian. This was understandable as he'd mentored him from a young age and Stephen was winning everything at that time. It was obvious that Stephen was the star of the stable but it never bothered me like it did some of the other players. Some of them couldn't understand it but I'd tell them that, to me, I was top dog, not Stephen, and that they should look at it the same way. A lot of other players just bitched about it because they didn't like the fact that Ian was the sort of character who liked the sound of his own voice. It annoyed a lot of players but that's just how he was. He was larger than life and players should have thought about what he was actually doing for them off the table, not what he was saying to the press.

I didn't always see it like that, however. When Steve Davis beat me 6-0 at Goffs in 1997 Ian called me a lazy bastard in the newspapers and said I didn't put the work in. That got my back up but he did me a favour because although it hurt and our relationship hit a low ebb as a result, it inspired me and I went on to win the World Championship. Ian knew what he was doing all along. He knew how to motivate his players, the things he could say to trigger the reaction he was looking for. He was meticulous as a manager, involving himself in every aspect of your career and your life, but he was good for me and I have much to thank him for. I don't always agree with everything Ian says but I like him a lot and we've had a great relationship. He has a good heart. He still loves snooker even though he's pretty much retired. I'm glad I signed for him.

My victory in the Welsh Open and encouraging performances in the other events meant that I joined the elite top 16 – the group of players excused from having to qualify for the major tournaments – after only three seasons on the tour. It meant I was no longer a member of the game's supporting cast but now a leading player in my own right. Now the other top players were looking at me more as an equal than a rising star.

With my confidence high and my career on the up and up, I set my sights on achieving every snooker professional's dream: winning the World Championship.

CHAPTER SEVEN

TALKING A GOOD GAME

Glasgow, 13 October 2009

I'm here in Glasgow for the Grand Prix final. Sadly, I'm not playing in it but since last season I've become a regular member of the BBC team and have been commentating and giving my opinions in the studio all week.

I did, however, qualify for this tournament with wins over Paul Davies and Dave Harold so I'm four wins out of four at Prestatyn this campaign, after losing all four of my matches there last season. Then for round one I drew Mark Selby. It was a tough draw because outside of Ronnie O'Sullivan and John Higgins he's in that category with the likes of Shaun Murphy, Neil Robertson and Stephen Maguire who are very dangerous and can win any tournament they play in. Mark's a very tough competitor. He beat me 6-5 in the semi-finals of the Masters last season and it really hurt because I'd lost two finals at Wembley and I felt it was a good chance for me to finally win the game's most prestigious invitation title.

So it was a tough match to get in the first round but what I've realised from being at the qualifiers is that you don't care who you draw once you make it through to a proper venue. You're just delighted to be in the tournament. I was so happy at being in the main draw that I wasn't edgy at all and managed to beat Mark 5-3, which was a great win for me.

Last season I couldn't do anything at all but winning matches in the qualifiers has given me loads of confidence for when I get to the venues. It proves that snooker is largely psychological. All the top professionals are talented and we can all play but you have to shut out all the negative thoughts and play with a clear mind. If you get on a run of bad results it is very hard to get off it again. The flipside of that coin is that if you do start winning again it becomes a habit every bit as much as losing was.

I'm not going to get carried away and say I'm back to my best but I've certainly improved on last season. It would be hard to be any worse. Wins over the likes of Mark Selby and any leading player give me something to build on. I feel like I'm climbing the hill back to the top. It's difficult but hopefully I'll make it.

My brother Anthony phoned me when I was in Shanghai and asked me how I got on against Neil Robertson. I told him I'd won and he was made up. Then he rang me again after I'd played Barry Hawkins and again I was able to tell him I'd won. He was so excited, it was like I'd just turned professional once more, because in some ways I was having to start all over again. I'd fallen so low that nobody had any expectations as to how I'd do and my supporters were genuinely thrilled that it looked like I was starting to turn a corner. All the lads in Anthony's work were asking how I was getting on and he said it was like going back 20 years, having that excitement back and not taking any results for granted. I feel like I've come full circle and that's certainly true psychologically. I was on a high for so many years then last season I hit an all-time low. Now, I feel I'm building myself back up again and feeling a lot happier about my snooker.

Back in Glasgow, Neil Robertson beat me 5-2 in the second round, which is why I'm now on BBC duties. They first approached me a couple of years ago. I was at the World Championship and it's such a long tournament that you can win on the Sunday and then not play again until the following Friday, so you have ages to hang around. Before a tournament a player might practise for five or six hours a day but the maximum you would put in during an event is an hour a day, so that leaves a lot of time just sitting in the players' room watching the matches on TV or trying to find other things to occupy your time. So when the BBC asked me if I'd like to spend an afternoon as a studio pundit I jumped at the chance. I thought it would be fun and, apart from anything else, it was just something to do.

I like watching snooker anyway and I found myself enjoying it. The BBC asked me to join the team the following year but at the time I was close to becoming world no.1 and I didn't feel I should detract from my playing. This season, I knew that being outside the top 16 meant I couldn't be guaranteed to be at the final stages of all the tournaments, so I agreed to be a full time member of the team apart from when I was playing. They were fine with that so I signed up.

Working for the BBC is stimulating because snooker remains a fascinating game whether you are playing or talking about it. They also cover all of the biggest tournaments, including the World Championship, so there is a real sense of occasion whenever the cameras go on or the microphones go live.

I didn't feel doing the BBC work had an adverse effect on my game here in Glasgow. It doesn't take that much out of you and it's not like I had anything else to do. I asked Steve Davis, who has been a BBC pundit for several years, whether he thought the TV work had affected his game. He said it hadn't and that it filled time when otherwise he might have been bored. If I wasn't commentating or doing the studio work I'd probably just be watching the snooker anyway. If I do get back in the top 16 I might change my mind because my playing career comes first but at the moment it's a nice way to stay involved with the game after I've been knocked out of a tournament.

One of the difficulties in being a TV pundit is that you sometimes have to criticise players and then face up to them later. That's one of the reasons Steve, John Parrott and I don't slate players too much. The other is that we've all been successful players and we know that playing snooker is much easier from the commentary box or studio. You have to remember how hard the game is and cut the players some slack. Ultimately, though, we're employed to give an opinion and that's what the viewers expect from us. The players usually understand it if they are publicly criticised because they know where they've messed up and how they've gone wrong and all we're doing is pointing this out to the public at large. Commentators and pundits and analysts have had a go at me over the years but you have to be man enough to either accept the criticism or disagree politely. I've never gone overboard on a player but there are times when you just have to say it as it is. The public aren't stupid. They know when they are being soft-soaped by pundits who won't come out and say what they think.

The job of an analyst is to explain to the viewers what a player is thinking and what he should – and shouldn't – be doing. You can't duck it. If something happens that demands your opinion then you have to give it. Otherwise there's no point being there at all. One of my first appearances in the BBC studio was at the 2005 World Championship when Peter Ebdon beat Ronnie O'Sullivan in a controversial quarter-final, in which Ebdon slowed down to a snail's pace and got under Ronnie's skin so badly that he lost the plot big time. He went to pieces because he couldn't handle Ebdon's tactics, which were beyond fair play. He was really dragging it out. At one point he took five minutes to make a break of 12, which was ridiculous. In my opinion the referee or tournament director should have stepped in and said something because it was outrageous.

What Peter did was within the rules but John and I, as players, were very critical of him, as were many members of the public. I think we were right to be. We couldn't sit on that couch and just trot out clichés. We had to say it as it was and be honest. The worst thing you can do is to act all nice in the studio and then say the exact opposite the minute the cameras are turned off. The viewers wouldn't stand for that and quite rightly. You shouldn't go over the top but you are paid to say what you think.

I enjoy the studio work more than the commentary. I find sitting in the commentary box tougher because there's no respite from it. Once the match starts there's no let-up but I do like working with the other commentators because they are all good guys: Willie Thorne, John Virgo and Dennis Taylor. I have a good laugh with them even if I don't always agree with what they say. I don't know what they think of me as a newcomer but we seem to have fun and they've been very welcoming. They have some great anecdotes about the old days, even if you do hear them over and over again. It's a good team and I think we bounce off each other well.

It was easy for me to fit in because I'd always enjoyed listening to the BBC commentators, including John and Dennis. I liked Willie as well, even though sometimes he can be too critical. At least he's honest and he calls the game well. Clive Everton is a great commentator who has authority and integrity and he is never biased towards any particular player.

The thing about commentary is that the experience depends on the quality of the match. If it's a really high standard then you become involved in every ball but if it gets dragged out then it's a struggle to retain concentration and make it sound interesting.

Willie is a great guy but can be a nightmare at times. Here

in Glasgow he had the *X-Factor* on one of the screens, then he switched to Sky News, then we're live for the final and it completely threw me because I didn't know where we were or where to look. You'd be watching the snooker and he'd turn the microphone off and slate one of the singers, saying she'll be a certainty to be voted off. Life with the Great WT has its moments but one thing he said to me was absolutely true. He told me that it's amazing what you can learn about snooker watching from the commentary box. He has a good insight into the game and notices things about the players that can be useful for other players.

Last season I commentated with Willie at the Crucible on the conclusion of the world final between John Higgins and Shaun Murphy. At one point John was leading 16-8 so I asked the executive producer, Graham Fry, if he'd prefer someone more experienced to commentate. I was only supposed to do the first four frames, but it was clear the final could end before the interval and this would be the biggest moment of the whole season. I was mindful that I was only a rookie but Graham said that if he didn't think I could do it he wouldn't have me there, which was nice to hear. John won 18-9 so I was on air as the match finished.

I enjoyed it but had mixed emotions because as I watched John and Shaun introduced into the arena my mind went back 12 years to when I won it, and then to 1998 when I played John in the final. I was thinking, 'Jeez, I wish I was back out there.' All the memories came flooding back. It got to Willie too. He was in tears at the end of the final when John brought his wife and kids out to celebrate with him. It made me emotional as well because just being there was so special, seeing John winning the trophy that I'd won. Commentating on it was nowhere near as good as playing in a world final but being in that arena, even if it was in a soundproof box, beat sitting at home watching on the TV.

I'm still learning as a commentator. I didn't really have much training; I was just thrown into it and I'm still finding my feet. Thankfully I haven't had any players coming up to me angry about something I've said. Not yet, anyway. But I'm not afraid of anyone challenging me. If they think I was wrong I can accept that. It's about opinions ultimately and you'll hear far worse when watching in the players' room.

Nothing beats being out there playing so being a BBC pundit will always rank second to that but it's something I've taken to and enjoy. Like the other guys on the team I love the game and want to stay involved in any way I can. Talking a good game – or a bad one – is a pretty satisfying substitute for being out in the middle.

CHAPTER EIGHT

KING OF THE CRUCIBLE

I'd never really done much in the World Championship before I won the title in 1997. Like everyone else in the game it was the one event I cherished, the one title I coveted above all the others, but it only comes round once a year and is very difficult to win.

To explain how special it is: it's like our FA Cup or Wimbledon or Open Golf Championship. It's the tournament everyone wants to win. There's so much history associated with it and so many memories that remain long after those from other events have faded. If you win the World Championship you know you will be remembered forever. It's the absolute pinnacle of snooker, our Holy Grail, and that all adds to the nerves and the excitement when you pitch up in Sheffield for the annual green baize marathon.

The annual pilgrimage to the Crucible comes at the end of our season but the excitement starts to grow as you get past Christmas and play in the tournaments building up to the big one. You need plenty of attributes to become world champion beyond mere skill at snooker. You need stamina, as the tournament is played over 17 days. You need self-belief and resilience, mental fortitude and a little bit of luck.

For a boy who dreamed of winning the title after watching Alex Higgins's success in 1982, just to play at the Crucible felt amazing, but then the reality sets in. Playing snooker is my career and, as in any career, you want to achieve the best that you can. Having lost to Steve Davis in my first season in 1991, I missed out for the next two years before losing 13-10 to Jimmy White in the quarter-finals in 1994.

The following year I suffered a huge disappointment when Mark Davis beat me 10-7 in the first round and then in 1996 I was beaten 13-5 by Darren Morgan in the second round. I was doing well in other tournaments but felt I hadn't achieved anything close to what I should have done in the one that really mattered. There were many talented players who had fallen short at the Crucible. I was determined not to be one of them.

In 1997, I drew Mark Davis in the first round again. It had been two years since he beat me but the memories were fresh in my mind and I didn't want to play him. It was a really tough encounter which I just managed to win 10-8. I sometimes look back to that match and wonder where my career would have gone had Mark beaten me again. Would I ever have been world champion or would I have slipped back and become one of the also-rans, perhaps demotivated and unsure whether I really had what was required to win the big one? That's how big a match it was in the context of my career.

I hadn't gone to Sheffield with much confidence, hardly any in fact, and I wasn't looking forward to it. Davis had beaten me heavily in both the Wembley and Irish Masters, and Michael Judge had beaten me in the first round of the British Open just before the World Championship. My game just didn't seem to be there and the results weren't coming. It happens to all players at all levels. You get dragged into these little troughs where you can't seem to win a match and you have to summon all your willpower to haul your way out of it. That's what my victory over Mark seemed to herald. I could easily have lost that match and that would have been my season over in the most disappointing fashion imaginable, followed by a miserable summer of sulking and then coming into the next season low on confidence and not in the right frame of mind to arrest the decline.

As it transpired, winning that match perked me up a bit. I'd avoided another first-round exit and my confidence rose a little. In the second round I was drawn to play Steve Davis, who had handed out those two hammerings in the previous months, and beat him 13-3 with a session to spare. It was funny because when I led 5-1 Steve did something I'd never seen him do before. He won a tight frame, came back to his chair, clenched his fist and went 'Yes!' as if to say, 'I'm back. This is the start of my comeback.' I thought, 'Well, fuck you. I'm not taking that. I'm still winning the match.' I got the bit between my teeth after that and started to play really well, winning eight of the next nine frames to clinch victory. It was probably the best snooker I had ever played and to do it against Steve, the all-conquering king of the Crucible in the 1980s – someone I'd gone to watch as a spectator back in 1984 and then played on my debut in 1991 – made it all the sweeter. It sent a message to everyone, myself included, that I could win the title.

In the quarter-finals I was up against John Higgins. John had broken through a few years earlier and was becoming a consistent winner of tournaments. He had become the first player to win three ranking titles while still a teenager, a record later emulated by Ding Junhui. John was still only 21 in 1997 but he had a maturity that meant he could mix Stephen Hendry's attacking game with Steve Davis's tactical nous. It made for quite an imposing package.

We had a good, hard match. John led 3-0. I pulled it back to 4-4 after the first session, led 9-7 going into the final session and eventually won 13-9. I guess at the quarter-final stage most people would have been predicting a Hendry–Higgins final. Certainly at that point John looked like he might be the player to take over from Hendry at the top of the rankings – something he accomplished a year later when he beat me in the Crucible final to win the first of his world titles.

Beating John was the final shot of confidence I needed to truly believe I could win the Championship. The fact that I'd had such a poor run in to Sheffield didn't matter any more. I had my sights set firmly on that famous old silver trophy and felt I was playing well enough to beat anyone.

In the semi-finals I beat Alain Robidoux of Canada 17-7 with a session to spare. I had to be careful not to take Alain for granted because, by this stage of the tournament, I was a heavy favourite to beat him but he was a tough match player and a wily old fox. He shared a lot of traits with Cliff Thorburn, another Canadian, who was world champion in 1980. Alain was an intelligent player and could trap you in all sorts of trouble if you weren't wise to the way he played. Our first session was closely fought and ended 4-4, but after that I started to pull away. I won seven of the eight frames in the second session to lead 11-5 before winning the third 6-2 to finish it off without having to come back for the final session. This must have been a help because it meant I could relax whereas Stephen Hendry had been involved in a close semi-final with James Wattana.

Well, I say I could relax but the reality was that I was so excited about playing Stephen in a world final that I couldn't sleep. However, this wasn't through fear of playing him. I always enjoyed coming up against Stephen, even when he beat me heavily. I actually had a pretty decent record against him. He didn't intimidate me and instead I tended to raise my own game whenever we played. I knew it would be tough because he hadn't lost at the Crucible in five years but I thought, 'Just go out there, enjoy the experience. You have nothing to lose because you're not expected to win.'

The way to beat Hendry was to outplay him tactically. You didn't have to outscore him or play him at his own game but try to stop him scoring, because when he got in he was absolutely lethal. The way to play him was to be clever. He didn't enjoy the safety side of the game so I knew my best chance of winning was with good matchplay snooker. I was also genuinely glad I was playing Stephen in the final because I knew if I'd played anyone else and won the title it would have been tarnished by the fact the best player in the world was already out. Nobody could say that, if I beat Hendry, I didn't deserve to be world champion.

After the first session I was 5-3 up. Stephen had won his three frames with century breaks but, overall, he wasn't playing as well as he could. I know that sounds strange but, apart from those big breaks, it was clear there was something up with him. He didn't have that focus he always had on major occasions, the aura of invincibility that was his trademark. He just wasn't himself. I thought, 'If I can get on top of him, I might be able to pull away' and I played on his weaknesses. His long game wasn't working like it normally did so I played some good safety, tempting him into taking on long balls which he would miss to let me in.

I won some great frames in the second session to forge 11-5 ahead by the end of the first day, just seven frames from the title. In one frame I doubled the re-spotted black and we both went to the toilet afterwards. While we were in there he said to me, 'I knew you'd get that,' which was a strange thing to say because he wouldn't normally get involved in any chat during a big match. I just replied, 'You should never leave a mug a double.'

Ian Doyle told the press that if Hendry wasn't careful he could lose the final with a session to spare. Ian was in the enviable position of having both finalists signed to his management stable so he couldn't lose, but it was also his job to try and inspire Stephen. I understood that but Hendry was fuming. He got the hump big time with Ian because he felt he was rubbing it in. He was already a long way behind and there was his manager telling journalists he was headed for humiliation. It was the best thing that could have happened for me because it infuriated Stephen and I pulled away to lead

15-7 before he won the last two frames of the afternoon to leave me 15-9 up and three frames from victory.

I went back to the hotel and carried out the routine that had held me in good stead up to this point, which was to go down to the swimming pool, swim around and just try to relax. It took my mind off snooker and meant I didn't have to talk to anyone or listen to the chat that you get around a tournament venue. But when I got back to the Crucible the nerves well and truly set in. I realised that this was the biggest night of my life. It was now or never: I was on the verge of achieving greatness but I was well aware of Hendry's powers of recovery. He'd done it to Jimmy White in the world final and to many other players at various tournaments. He was capable of doing it to me.

In my mind, I was thinking that if I could have won one of the last two frames of the previous session and been 16-8 ahead that probably would have been enough to stem the nerves. Though still a handsome lead, 15-9 didn't quite seem so insurmountable. I was trying to keep my confidence up by telling myself, 'He has to beat me 9-2 to win this thing.' It seemed unlikely but I knew it wasn't impossible and if anyone could do it, Stephen could.

I was nervous when we were introduced back into the arena for the last time. I just couldn't help it. This was my moment, the point of no return, and it was up to me not to screw it up. I started off a bit shaky and Stephen won the first frame of the evening and then made a century – his fifth of the final – to close to 15-11. In the next, I was 50-odd ahead and went for a red with the rest, missed and careered into the pack of reds, opening them for him. He won the frame in two visits and suddenly it was 15-12.

In frame 28 I was 30 or so ahead and Stephen got in with a chance to dish up. There was a red on the top cushion and he went for it, but it hung in the jaws of the corner pocket. I jumped out of my chair like a greyhound because I only needed a red and a colour. I potted them and it made it 16-12 instead of 15-13. It was the last frame before the interval and had I lost that one as well, I would have spent the break sitting nervously in my dressing room, thinking about the fact I'd lost six on the spin and that my grip on the trophy was gradually loosening. As it was, I had some much-needed breathing space and the pressure was slightly lifted. The truth is that I was starting to freeze but getting to 16-12 gave me a new impetus and I won the next frame as well to make it 17-12.

In frame 30 he had a chance but missed a red down the side cushion. I snookered him, he failed to hit the red and I cleared up to win the match and the title. It was the most amazing feeling in the world. I looked over to see Tony Drago in the press seats, clapping like a seal. I had a dozen or so friends over from Dublin and I'd had to ignore them before the final because I just wanted to concentrate on the match. But we had a party that night.

It was unbelievable. It was everything I'd ever wanted. Here, on the Crucible stage, holding the World Championship trophy up in the air, just like Alex Higgins had, just like all the greats had, surrounded by the cameras and the acclaim from the audience. To have beaten the great Stephen Hendry made it all the more special and he was very gracious afterwards. It was all a lot to take in at that moment but, somewhere inside, I think I realised that my life had changed forever.

CHAPTER NINE

SENIORS SERVICE

Glenrothes, 1 November 2009

I turned 40 in September and that means I'm now eligible for seniors snooker. That seems absurd because it only feels like yesterday that I was coming over to Britain as a teenager to try my luck, but it's now official: I'm one of the game's old gits.

Snooker doesn't yet have a seniors circuit like they do in golf and tennis, which is a shame because there would be a big market for it. People still ask after the players they remember from the 1980s when the sport was even bigger than football for a time in terms of television ratings. When Dennis Taylor potted that black to pip Steve Davis 18-17 in the 1985 World Championship final there were 18.5 million viewers watching, even though it was gone midnight. Many other finals and matches in the 1980s pulled in audiences of more than 10 million so the players really were household names and some were superstars.

My management company, 110sport, has set up an internet channel to stream snooker tournaments and one of them is the Legends event, which has been held here in Glenrothes in Fife over the past two days. It was going to be called Seniors rather than Legends but Stephen Hendry, who is a few months older than me, said he wouldn't play in it if it was. They brought eight players in – myself, Stephen, Jimmy White, Alex Higgins, Cliff Thorburn, Tony Knowles, Tony Drago and Nigel Bond – and I lost 5-3 to Hendry in the final.

It's a great idea and was genuine fun getting some of the old boys together again and having a laugh about the old days. There was plenty of nostalgia around and it was fascinating to hear stories from players like Cliff and Jimmy about professional snooker in the early 1980s, when I was glued to it on the TV.

For all the fun we had backstage, once the matches began it was clear everyone was taking it seriously. That competitive instinct kicked in. You don't lose that, even if you haven't played professionally for some years, as in the case of Cliff and Alex. It's the same for any sportsperson. Whatever we are doing we want to compete and, ideally, win. It's all about giving your best.

I watched some of these players as a kid and was a little in awe of them, hanging on their every word. Alex was well behaved, although at times a little off the wall. At one point he threw money over his head and tried to land it in a pint glass across the bar. That's Alex. You never really know what he's going to do next but that's why so many people still follow him. He has some great one-liners. When Tony first came over from Malta he was as skinny as a rake. He's enjoyed a good few meals since then and when a journalist asked how he was still as fast as he was 20 years ago, Alex described him as 'a gazelle in a buffalo's body'.

He and Cliff Thorburn don't get on. They are different characters and Alex, as most people know, is a combustible sort who can start a row with anyone. We were sat in the hotel the day before the Legends tournament began and I was with Alex and Jimmy. I looked round and saw Cliff coming in. He clocked Alex and they were looking at one another, not knowing what to do or whether to say hello to each other. In the end, Alex got up and went over to shake Cliff's hand, which broke the ice. Cliff beat him 4-0 in the first round and got very emotional afterwards because he had in his mind the Alex Higgins of old and had been confronted by how frail he had become, hardly able to speak because of his throat cancer and a shadow of his former self on the table.

I was impressed by Cliff. He's elegant, professional and always the perfect gentleman. He was always the housewives' favourite, even though his style of play was quite slow. He was gritty and determined but a great sportsman. Cliff has the driest wit and is very funny, which isn't something a lot of people will know if they haven't encountered him away from the table. He told one story about how he'd lost a qualifying match at Blackpool towards the end of his career and a fan came up to him and started going through the entire match, telling him where he had gone wrong. Cliff listened for a while then turned to him and said, 'Excuse me, but I think you're confusing me with someone who gives a fuck.'

We got more than 500 people in watching the final, which made for a really good atmosphere. It was nice to get to that stage of a tournament again and to play Stephen. The last time I'd played him in a final was in Thailand in 2001, when I beat him 9-3 to win the ranking tournament there. His game is a bit up and down these days, as mine is, but he played well to win. Like me, he still wants more from the game, despite his unparalleled record of success in the modern era.

I don't see any reason why seniors snooker shouldn't be successful. OK, the standard of play drops as you get older and your consistency goes, so you are less capable of stringing together a series of strong performances day after day. But there are a number of players, Stephen Hendry and myself included, who are still producing good snooker on our day on the pro circuit. Several other top players who are still playing professionally are at that stage where they are turning 40, such as Peter Ebdon, Alan McManus and James Wattana, so a seniors circuit could become a genuine entity in the next couple of years. Joe Johnson, another former world champion, is promoting a World Seniors Championship next season, which I think will be popular.

I hope so. So many of these veteran players have played a part in getting snooker to the point where it has a professional circuit and the fans want to see them, speak to them, get photos and autographs, and generally pay tribute to them as legends of the sport. It gives the public a chance to reminisce and it's something different to the established tournaments.

Also, the older players are very good at interacting with the public because it was part of their training in the days when there was very little money in tournament snooker and they toured holiday camps and the exhibition circuit to make ends meet. Part of that was developing a bit of patter, doing jokes and trick-shots and generally entertaining.

You get all sorts of aches and pains as you get older, but snooker isn't a physical sport so there's no reason why you can't keep playing to some sort of standard when you're no longer a spring chicken. Steve Davis has proved that by remaining in the top 32 into his fifties.

You need motivation to keep practising and seniors tournaments provide that. It feels strange to be in this bracket now. I certainly don't feel like a senior citizen but, in snooker terms, I guess I am.

CHAPTER TEN

THE NIGHTMARE MISS

There are some shots people always remember and they are usually misses. It stems from the expectation we all have when watching top players: that they will finish the job they've started, so if they've created a chance to make a match-winning clearance or a big break, they will complete the task. We've all seen them do that many times over but have also witnessed some howlers that stay with a player regardless of any other success they enjoy.

Willie Thorne, for instance, was a brilliant player who won titles but people always associate him with a blue off its spot he missed when leading Steve Davis 13-8 in the 1985 UK Championship final. It turned the whole match and Willie ended up losing 16-14. It seemed to cast him in the public consciousness as a nearly-man who had bags of talent but maybe not the poise under pressure.

Even Steve, for all his incredible success, is known for the black he missed against Dennis Taylor at the end of their epic 1985 World Championship final. In case anyone needs reminding, Steve led 8-0 before Dennis fought back to 17-17. The decider lasted more than an hour before Dennis potted brown, blue and pink to take the match and the destination of the famous trophy down to the very last ball. After several attempts on each side, Steve was left with a cut-back to a corner pocket, the sort of pot that is missable but one everyone expected the great man to make. It jawed and left the door open for Dennis to knock the black in, probably the most famous pot in snooker history considering the record 18.5 million post-midnight viewing audience on BBC2.

The greatest of all time, Stephen Hendry, missed a re-spotted black against Mark Williams in the deciding frame of their 1998 Masters final. It was by no means an easy pot but it left Williams a pretty straightforward one, which he slotted home to clinch the title. For all Stephen has won, it must still rankle, particularly as it is still shown on TV now and again.

My own worst miss – and there have been more than a few in a professional career now into its third decade – came at Wembley Conference Centre in 2000. The Benson and Hedges Masters was one of our most prestigious events. It still is, even though we were forced to get rid of tobacco firms as sponsors in 2003 because of government legislation. We also had to move to Wembley Arena in 2007 because the old venue was demolished as part of the stadium redevelopment. Despite this, the Masters remains an annual highlight on the snooker calendar. The tournament doesn't carry ranking points and is all about prestige and big money. It's only open to the top 16 in the world plus two wildcards, so you know it's all about the elite.

I reached the final for the first time in 1999, when I led John Higgins 8-6 and played really well, only for him to beat me 10-8. A year later I was back in the final against Matthew Stevens, who had started to challenge for major titles on a regular basis in the previous 18 months. He would go on to reach the Crucible final that year and again in 2005 but finish runner-up each time. He appeared in three semi-finals at Sheffield in between but never won the title, which was almost as much a surprise as Jimmy White failing to scoop the big one. In fact, Matthew's only ranking title success so far came at the 2003 UK Championship, but he was a formidable player and I'm pleased to see him get some form back after entering a slump a few years ago.

I trailed Matthew 9-5 in the final, so he needed one more frame for victory. At the start of the next frame, he went in-off and left me a long red. I could have run it in, come off the top cushion and played for the blue or baulk colours with an element of safety in mind but the reds were nicely open so I decided to try and get on the black. At that point, the chances of me winning the final were receding. I hadn't given up but I knew victory was unlikely so I just wanted to make a big break and at least go down in style.

I knocked the red in, got on the black and started to make the break. I felt good as I did. They were all there for me and I potted 15 reds with 15 blacks, then the yellow, a really good green, a good brown, the blue and then an awkward pink with the rest. The black wasn't dead straight but wasn't one you should ever miss really. It was one of those shots where you can't quite get comfortable. The cue ball was fairly close to the cushion and I couldn't decide whether to put my bridge hand on the top of the cushion or on the bed of the table because neither felt quite right. In the end, I put it on the cushion but I missed the black and therefore failed to make a 147, which would have been my first and only the second in the history of the Masters. The prize was a lovely sports car worth something like £90,000. It was parked in the foyer of the Conference Centre and I'd pass it every morning. Each time I'd think, 'I'd love to own that.' And I got so close...

The first televised maximum break was made by Steve Davis in 1982. Cliff Thorburn made the first one at the Crucible a year later and in 1984 Kirk Stevens, in his famous white suit, completed a 147 at the Masters. By 2000 they were starting to become more common but were still a big deal, especially on television and especially in a major final.

I suppose I must have missed the black through nerves or pressure or whatever label you want to give it. The Conference Centre held nearly 3,000 spectators, quite a few of whom were Irish and supporting me, and the atmosphere was amazing. The crowd were roaring on every pot as I got to the colours and the noise created a kind of electricity that ran through my body. It was like a wave of emotion that I was riding. I was shaking beyond belief but the balls were still going in.

I didn't hit the pink as I wanted to and finished high on the black. My arms and legs were trembling. I could barely stand up, let alone get down to try and pot the black. Instead of just rolling it in I decided to try and stun it in. Everything seemed to happen in slow motion. I got down over the cue ball and could see the audience start to stand up all around me. Then it fell silent. It felt like an out of body experience. I could see myself, in that arena, on the black. But it didn't go in. The black stayed out.

I didn't know what to do. I couldn't move. I had nothing left in my legs. I sat down in my chair and although I wanted to go out of the arena, I literally couldn't get up. I wanted to cry but couldn't even do that because all the emotion had drained out of me. I was completely punch-drunk, like a boxer who has been hammered for 12 rounds and doesn't know where he is by the end of it.

It wasn't only me who couldn't believe I'd missed it. There were gasps all round the Conference Centre from the crowd, although they all still stood up and applauded me. It left me numb and I've no idea how I managed to play on. I won the next frame but, just to rub salt into the wound, lost the final 10-8, so it was like a double whammy.

It was, I suppose, an unmissable black, but that doesn't factor in the tension of what the moment means to a player. Had it been the first frame of the first round I probably would have got it but the pressure was magnified by the occasion. My back arm was shaking as I got down to play the black because I had an acute awareness of what it all meant and how big a deal it would be if I potted it. Nothing I could have done would have stopped that. My arms and legs didn't feel like my own and the cue might as well have been a broomstick. That's what pressure does to you.

It didn't really sink in on the night but over time it has become the source of my biggest ever disappointment. I still have nightmares about it: genuine times when I wake up in the middle of the night thinking about the black and how I missed it. I picture myself potting it but obviously that's all in vain now. It's on YouTube and I have a look at it every now and again just to really do my head in.

The next morning, a newspaper took me to a snooker club in London and lined up the same shot on the black. I had to play it ten times to see how many I would get or miss. Needless to say, I potted them all. It was nonsense and didn't prove anything. To this day I've got no idea why I agreed to do it. It must rank as one of the worst decisions of my life. The last thing I wanted to do was see that pot again, yet there I was, playing it over and over again. Each time it went in I felt worse because I was thinking, 'Why couldn't I have done that last night?' The paper was saying they could get me a car anyway, but of course that turned out to be a load of rubbish.

The next tournament was in Malta the following week. I was in the practice room when Stephen Hendry came in, took one look at me and said, 'Shouldn't you be practising blacks off the spot?' After missing like that I knew I could expect a bit of ribbing, but the funny thing was that I went on to win that Malta ranking event, beating Mark Williams 9-3 in the final. Maybe it fired me up, like I had something to get out of my system.

The funny thing is that people, for some reason, assume I've forgotten all about it, so they approach me and say things like, 'Do you remember the black you missed for a 147 at Wembley that time?' You feel like replying, 'No, I don't remember that at all.' The truth is that it's followed me round and always will do. Whenever a player is on a 147 on TV it's not long before one of the commentators will say, 'Now, don't do what Ken Doherty did in that Masters final and miss the black.' It never goes away. It's just torture.

I suppose the only way to get past it is to make one on TV, preferably in the World Championship where there is a £147,000 cash bonus for a maximum. Even then, though, I reckon people would still remember the one I missed.

I'll never get over it. I know people will talk about me winning the World Championship and various other tournaments but they'll also mention the black. It's one of those snooker moments that seems to be remembered long after many others have been forgotten. One of the reasons is the importance of the occasion. The Masters final is a big showpiece event and millions of people were watching on television. It would have been a great time to make a maximum but there were few worse ones to miss the final black.

I've still never made a 147 in professional competition and it would have been a significant achievement. I'd rather be world champion than make a maximum but it would have been a real feather in my cap. As it was, I was left with a horrible feeling and I still have it to this day. It's the one thing in my career I would want to go back in time and change, just to have that black again. And to pot it.

CHAPTER ELEVEN

ROBBED

Dublin, 19 November 2009

I've had many great moments following Manchester United but last night suffered one of the all-time lows watching Ireland.

It was the second leg of the World Cup qualifying play-off against France in Paris. Ireland needed to win 2-0 to go through to the finals in South Africa. I went to watch it in a pub here in Dublin with a few of my pals and it was a fantastic atmosphere, absolutely packed. Ireland were tremendous and played France off the park. They should have put the game to bed. And then towards the end France scored but it was clear from the replays that Thierry Henry had handled the ball not once but twice. It was about as blatant a piece of cheating as you will ever see. Except the referee didn't see it and the goal stood.

It was gut-wrenching because Ireland were cheated out of going to the World Cup finals. They played so well all night and didn't deserve that. The country was going through a bad time with the recession biting and a lot of people out of work. We needed a lift and being at the World Cup would have given us it. It would have been a real feel-good factor for the whole country.

I've always respected Henry as a player and an athlete. He's so skilful and has been a joy to watch over the years. The problem with football today is that cheating has become accepted as a part of the game but that's wrong – it shouldn't be like that. Henry obviously knew he'd done it so I've no idea why the linesman or referee didn't see it. What really got me was Henry's celebration after he knew he'd cheated. He'll be tarred for the rest of his career, which is a shame.

I know these things do happen but this was such an important match. Roy Keane says Ireland only have themselves to blame, but I think that's more to do with his deep-rooted attitude towards the F.A.I. after what happened at the 2002 World Cup, when he went home early. I admire Roy and defended him over that but it's out of order to have a go at Ireland about this. I think he just saw it as his chance to stick the boot in.

We're lucky in snooker, as they are in golf, in that we have a strong etiquette between the players which means that we own up to fouls, even if the referee hasn't spotted them. It's admirable and the complete opposite of football where players are constantly trying to gain an advantage by bending or at times breaking the rules. What worries me is that kids are influenced by the top players, their heroes, and they think that if Thierry Henry can do it, so can they in their junior matches.

The match looked like it was heading for penalties, where we would have had every chance, so the atmosphere in the pub went from one when everyone was on a high to decidedly grim. What happened in Paris has left many people in Ireland upset and disappointed. Sport often evokes these kinds of emotions but it's even worse when you lose because someone has cheated. I would never want to win anything in that way.

CHAPTER TWELVE

THE HURRICANE

My snooker hero growing up was Alex Higgins and I became proud to call him a friend. He was the reason I took up snooker. When he won the World Championship in 1982 it would be true to say it changed my life because I realised at that moment what I wanted to be. I wanted to be like Alex.

He was Irish, he was different, he was unpredictable and he played the game in a mesmerising way. The 'Hurricane' played shots nobody else would even attempt, never mind actually pull off. He was the most incredible sportsman I had ever seen.

Alex transformed snooker in the 1970s. After winning the world title in 1972 at the age of 23 in his first season as a professional, he went on to create the excitement and drama, the hype and the interest in the game, dragging in fans with his extraordinary charisma and playing style, and that was what the television companies wanted. It exploded into the big time in the 1980s off the back of Alex and his exploits. He inspired me and doubtless many other successful players not just to watch snooker on TV but to play it as well. He did more than anyone else to make it popular.

I was 15 when I first met Alex at Goffs in County Kildare where they used to hold the Irish Masters. Kevin Norton, the promoter, gave me a job as an usher, which was thrilling for me because I had a chance to see what happened at a tournament up close and meet some of the players. One of the first things Alex said to me was that if he asked me for an orange juice, it meant he wanted a vodka and orange. If he asked for a vodka and orange, that meant he wanted a double.

There was always an electricity around Alex. When he lost in the final there in 1985 he came into the players' room, which was where players and their guests and sponsors' representatives went to relax. There was usually a good atmosphere in there but when Alex walked in the whole place fell silent. All eyes were fixed on him. That's the aura he had. They didn't know what to expect from him, whether something would kick off, whether he'd be rude to someone or behave himself. You never knew and that remained the case right throughout his life.

I was there in 1989 when he won the Irish Masters by beating Stephen Hendry 9-8 in the final. Alex had suffered an accident a few weeks earlier and injured his ankle, so he was basically hopping around the table. It was incredible, really, but he was irrepressible like that. He would never accept adversity and often thrived on it. He could sell Goffs out several times over such was the demand for his matches. There were 744 seats – I remember the figure from my days as an usher – but there was standing room as well in the balconies. Alex played Dennis Taylor there in 1990 and there were something like 2,500 people crammed in the place. It was just electric. They had to resell the stubs of the tickets because they hadn't printed enough.

It was a match everyone wanted to see because the pair of them had had a major falling out, to put it mildly, a few weeks earlier. They'd been playing in the same Northern Ireland team in the World Cup. There was a disagreement over something and Alex threatened to have Dennis shot if he ever returned to Northern Ireland. The row was overheard by a few people, including John Spencer, who was the chairman of the governing body. It was the main reason Alex ended up being banned for a year at the end of the season. He was unrepentant. He said, 'I didn't threaten to have him shot. I said if I'd had a gun I'd shoot him myself.' I'm not sure how that made any difference but he seemed to think it did.

Alex was a firebrand but also very funny and intelligent. He was well read and could talk to you about any subject. We never had an argument, which probably puts me in a minority in the snooker world, but there was one incident that disappointed me.

It was just after I won the World Championship in 1997. Alex was in the newspapers because he'd been stabbed by his girlfriend and was living in a caravan. I suggested we held a testimonial night for him because he'd given the game so much and helped to establish snooker as a major TV attraction so players like me could make a good living from it. I thought we should give something back to him. The *Sunday World* newspaper got on board and we organised a night at the Waterfront Hall in Belfast, which was packed with more than 2,000 people. Alex came out wearing his trademark fedora and got a huge ovation.

We had a best of nine frames match, which went the distance, and the crowd seemed to love every minute. But – and there was so often a 'but' where Alex was concerned – he spoiled the night by refusing to sign any autographs. He was basically destitute and set to make around £30,000 from the evening. The *Sunday World* had already given him a cheque for £10,000 before the testimonial had even started. Our two dressing rooms were next to each other and he had a crate of champagne. He and his pals were swigging it back while I spent an hour and a half downstairs signing autographs on my own. Some of the punters were giving out because Alex wasn't there. They couldn't understand why, on a night built around him, he wouldn't come down and show his appreciation for the people who had come along to support him. They included a coach-load of people who had come up from Dublin and although everyone enjoyed the snooker, many left disappointed that they couldn't get an autograph or a picture of their hero.

I thought Alex was bang out of order over that. He bit the hand that fed him. The *Sunday World* had planned another big night for him at the Point in Dublin but after what happened in Belfast they said they'd never work with him again. He had no reason to act like that but it was typical of his self-destructive personality, which he was never really able to shake off. All he had to do was come downstairs and sign autographs for people who rightly regarded him as a legend but something inside told him that they could go shove it. It's hard for most people to understand but that was his character.

At the end of the night I was getting ready to leave for Dublin. I knocked on his dressing room door to say goodnight and he said, 'OK, babes, thanks for everything. We must do it again some time.' He was back to his cheery old self as if nothing had happened. The experience upset me at the time but I got over it. Alex was a lovable rogue and as long as you understood what he was like, then you could overlook all the other stuff. I didn't hold a grudge.

The first time I played him was at Stoke in the qualifiers for the 1991 UK Championship. He beat me 6-4. This was in the days when he could still play to a good standard. He was my idol and I was in awe of him. I couldn't believe I was actually playing him and it probably affected my focus on the match.

In 1994 I played Alex in the first round at the Crucible in what turned out to be his last appearance there. Not surprisingly, it proved to be a controversial one. The referee, John Williams, told me afterwards that Alex had come to him before the match and told him to always stand over his right shoulder so that Alex couldn't see him. During the match he got down to play one shot, John stood where he had been asked to and Alex told him to move. John stood his ground and said that he wasn't going to move, that he'd stood in the same place all day and that Alex should play and he'd referee.

Alex blamed John Williams for losing the match but whether he really believed that or not I don't know. It became a bit like watching John McEnroe play tennis: if there wasn't some flare-up you'd leave disappointed. Perhaps Alex played on that a bit. Nobody could ever accuse him of not being value for money. I'm not sure the referees quite saw it that way and I couldn't blame them for that. He once farcically accused Williams of 'standing in my line of thought'.

It was that sense of the unexpected that put everyone on edge. You just never knew what he was going to do, who he was going to have a go at or what was going to happen next. I heard a story from an exhibition where he'd told the referee he was useless and didn't know what he was doing. Alex took the referee's gloves off his hands, walked over to someone in the audience and said, 'You're the referee now.'

He did a lot of things in his career I couldn't agree with but it was extremely harsh to ban him for a whole year in 1990. They threw the book at him because he'd upset so many people and they wanted to get rid of him. They took all his ranking points away and it was basically the end of him, because he pretty much had to start all over again from scratch after his season out in the cold. Just before he was banned he'd got back into the top 16 and could have had several more years at the top of the game but as it was he ended up back at the qualifiers. I know that for the rest of his life he felt he had been done a great injustice.

I agree with him because there's a contrast with how Ronnie O'Sullivan has been dealt with over various things more recently. Ronnie's treatment has been far more lenient, which is inconsistent and unfair. I'm not saying Ronnie should have been banned for anything he's done but Alex was treated much more harshly.

However, Alex went through life as a rebel thinking the whole world was against him. One of his problems was that he never really accepted that there had been times when he'd been in the wrong. He even blamed the senior tournament official he headbutted in 1986, saying the official had been victimising him by asking him to take part in a drugs test, even though all players are asked to do one at various times. I don't know what the plant pot did to him that he had to urinate into it at the Crucible that time but he probably blamed it for being in his way as he went to the toilet. He just had that sort of temperament and it caused excitement but also trepidation for many on the circuit. The fans loved him but many behind the scenes breathed a huge sigh of relief every time he was knocked out of a tournament.

Alex died on 24 July 2010. I was in Thailand where I'd been playing in a six reds tournament with a lot of other well known players. I'd stayed on because I was going on to Hong Kong for an exhibition the following week.

I was out for the evening with Joe Swail, a professional from Belfast and very good friend of mine, as well as Mark Selby and his manager, Mukesh Parmar. We were having a drink, just chilling out, and Joe got a text from a friend who worked at the hospital Alex had been taken to. The text said he'd been pronounced dead. The first thought that came into my head was that it could be a wind-up, a sick joke. I tried to phone Alex but it just rang out. About 15 minutes later Jason

Francis, who organised a Snooker Legends tour that I played in, called to tell me that BBC Northern Ireland had been in touch because they'd heard a rumour Alex was dead. Then someone else rang and too many people seemed to have heard for it to be anything but true. I was devastated.

Everyone knew Alex was ill but he'd been written off so many times before that when he actually did die it came as a big shock. He'd looked terribly ill for the last ten years of his life but was such a great survivor that you thought he'd somehow make it. His big problem, though, was that he didn't eat. He'd beaten cancer but barely ate. His teeth were ruined and he could only eat blended baby food, which was sad beyond words. Money was raised for an operation for new teeth in Spain but he was apparently too ill to undergo surgery.

We were all in shock around the table, even though we knew Alex had been unwell. Joe had wandered into a pub in Belfast with his girlfriend a couple of months previously and spotted Alex. They went out for a few drinks around the town and he was good as gold but he rapidly declined in health.

The last time I saw Alex was at the Six Reds World Championship in Killarney in December 2009. We had an end of tournament dinner and Alex was sat out in the bar on his own, just reading the paper. I brought him into the room with everyone else. It was the week before Christmas and he was pulling crackers with everybody, but his throat cancer meant he could barely talk in anything above a whisper and in a crowded room you couldn't really make out what he was saying.

The next day I got the train back to Dublin, which Alex was

on. We played the card game kalooki and Alex won twenty or thirty quid off me but wouldn't take it, even though he could have done with it. That was what I was thinking about in that bar in Thailand. It was the last time I'd seen him, even though we'd spoken several times on the phone since. But there was so much more I'd like to have said to him and all of a sudden he was gone.

After I qualified for the 2010 World Championship I turned on my mobile and his was the first message of congratulations. I know he had run-ins with many people in his life but he could also be kind. I don't know why we got on so well. Maybe as he was my hero I couldn't see any bad in him. To me, some of the bad stuff was funny and I forgave him. I wish now we could have done more for him, but Alex was his own man and did things in his own way.

There was a huge turnout in Belfast for the funeral. The streets were lined with thousands of people – a fitting farewell for the people's champion. It was very sad but we celebrated his life. Beforehand, we went down to his family's house and they'd laid his fedora, the one he wore when he was introduced into the Crucible in 1994 to play me, on his coffin. It was very emotional but with his family and friends around him it proved he was loved. The funeral cortège was pulled by two slow horses, which was appropriate because he'd backed enough of those in his time. I'm sure he would have seen the funny side of that. I carried the coffin for part of the Hurricane's final journey, which I was proud but sad to do. The people clapped him every step of the way.

It was a beautiful service and Alex's daughter, Lauren, read out a moving poem she'd written herself. There was a good turnout of snooker players – Jimmy White, John Virgo, Willie Thorne, Tony Knowles, Tony Meo, Stephen Hendry, Eugene Hughes, Patsy Fagan, Shaun Murphy, Mark Selby and various Irish players. I was particularly full of admiration that Stephen Hendry came. He didn't have to be there, not least because Alex had once greeted him before a match by saying, 'Hello, I'm the Devil.' Stephen wasn't a close friend of Alex but it said a lot about him that he would come. He explained that Alex and Jimmy were the only top players who would practise with him when he was starting out and he wanted to repay that debt. He actually rang Jimmy and asked him if he thought Alex would have minded him going to the funeral. Jimmy said Alex would have been honoured and I think that's true. Whatever had been said in the past, he respected Stephen.

I was a bit disappointed that some other players didn't turn up. Snooker owed Alex Higgins a huge amount. He was a pioneer who brought a lot of attention to the game. When he first won the World Championship in 1972 it was played in a run-down British Legion club, there was no television coverage and he earned just £480. Ten years later when he won it for the second time, it was one of the biggest sports on TV, a multi-million-pound circuit was being established and the players were becoming household names. Alex was the main reason for that. He drew people to snooker and they loved the controversy as much as the extraordinary way he played the game. That's certainly true of me and of Stephen Hendry.

So I think more players and figures from that time who

earned a good living from snooker should have come to show their appreciation. Barry Hearn could have made an effort to come, as chairman of World Snooker and someone who knew Alex. I'm sure Dennis Taylor had his reasons – their relationship never fully recovered after Alex threatened to have him shot – but I think Steve Davis could have come. When someone dies the past should be forgotten. Maybe he didn't have respect for some players but they should still acknowledge him and what he did for snooker.

Alex was a one-off. He genuinely didn't care what people thought of him and would either take you or leave you. As far as he was concerned you could do the same with him. He liked me for some reason and in turn I enjoyed his company. He had the most incredible charisma and people seemed to love him. I remember one pub we went into where he ended up getting not only free drinks but also persuaded the landlady to put his bets on for him. That was the power he held over people. They warmed to him, even when he was doing things that were beyond the pale. The life I have now is largely down to Alex. I was instantly captivated by snooker when I saw it on TV but when I watched him play it became an addiction. I have a lot to thank him for.

Alex was 61 when he died. It's amazing really that Alex ever reached 60 when you think about the way he lived his life but he packed so much in it's like he lived two lifetimes. His life was like a rollercoaster – full throttle with plenty of ups and downs. I found it sad to see him reduced to the frail figure he was in his last years. He was so thin and could barely speak. The cancer left him looking much older than he actually was and he was a world away from the heroic figure I remember so vividly cutting a dash on TV when I was a boy.

Alex was such a star that he could have been the richest of all the snooker players but he chose a different life and one that was self-destructive. Throughout it all he remained unapologetic. He was a fantastic player, the most exciting there has ever been, and led a colourful, controversial life that the tabloids lapped up. It put snooker on the front pages and created a real buzz around the sport. Snooker went on without him but it missed his larger than life presence.

I can't defend everything he did but without all the drama and controversy he wouldn't have been Alex 'Hurricane' Higgins, the people's champion; and the public, his public, wouldn't have had him any other way.

CHAPTER THIRTEEN

FLYING HIGH

Although George Best and Alex Higgins are among my sporting heroes, I can't say that I share their lifestyles. Many sportsmen, particularly footballers, end up in the tabloids but that's not something that interests me. You won't see me falling out of a nightclub – not a fashionable one anyway – at three in the morning.

Yet there was one notorious incident that put me on the front page of every newspaper in Ireland. In 2006, the morning after I won the Malta Cup, a ranking title, John Higgins and myself were ordered off the flight back home. Headlines screamed of drunkenness and it must have looked to everyone as if we had behaved very badly. Much was written about it when it happened – now it's time for me to have my say and explain what really went on.

It was a classic case of going from ecstasy and elation to the pits of despair within 24 hours. First, the happy part of the story. Malta was my first appearance in a ranking event final since I'd lost 18-16 to Mark Williams in the World Championship three years earlier. I knew it would be a tough match against John, because it always is, but I was 5-2 up after the first session and feeling good. I thought if I could win three of the first four frames of the evening session then the match would basically be over but because it had been a while since I'd been involved in a final I got a little nervous and he came back at me, winning six frames in a row to lead 8-5.

Then a funny thing happened. John was on 40 odd needing just a few more balls to beat me 9-5 but he missed a red. It was most unlike him because he usually finishes off a match in style, but it let me back in. I made a miraculous clearance and from then on played really good, solid stuff. He broke off at 8-8, left me a long red, I banged it in and made one of the best half-century breaks I've ever made to leave him needing snookers. To beat someone of John's calibre by winning the last four frames felt like a great achievement and it was made all the more satisfying because it was my first ranking event victory for five years.

We did the press conference, went on to the official reception and then across the road from the hotel to a little bar where we had a few drinks. I'm good friends with John and as we were the only players left in Malta, it was natural that we would celebrate and commiserate together whatever the result of the final. We went on to a nightclub, and my mate Mick McLean and I left at about 4am. The bus was coming to pick us up at 5am for a 7am flight. I'd had a few drinks but certainly wasn't roaring drunk, just merry. I'd already packed so I just laid my head down and then went down to get the bus.

John had come back from the nightclub later than me and basically got his gear and headed to the airport without any sleep. He looked the worse for wear but was on good form and we were having a laugh while we waited for the flight. He was obviously still intent on drowning his sorrows because he went up to the airport bar and ordered a pint. It wasn't even 6am at this point but I'd like to make it clear that although John was drunk, he wasn't being obnoxious or rude. He just didn't know when to stop, and this would cost him an hour or so later.

It was all good fun. We weren't being rowdy but when we went to get on the bus to take us to the plane, John's foot got stuck in the door and I think that alerted some of the other passengers to the fact he was drunk. They had to open the door for him to get his foot out. We were all laughing at him but maybe this didn't go down well either. I got on the plane and took my seat. Mick sat beside me. John was one of the last to get on. He just sort of staggered to his seat. I saw one of the passengers point to him and one of the stewards came over to him and said, 'Sorry, we can't let you on the flight.' When he asked them why they said they could see he was drunk and were worried that he could cause problems on the flight. He kept telling them that he just wanted to have a sleep and wouldn't be any trouble but they weren't having it, so he shouted over to me and asked me to have a word. So I got up and explained that, yes, he'd had a few drinks but that he'd be asleep in minutes and wouldn't cause any problems for anyone. I told them not to serve him any drink and just let him sit down. John is a bit of a comic drunk and he couldn't have caused any disruption even if he'd wanted to.

Then the captain came out and told John he would have to get off the flight before turning to me and telling me I'd have to join him. I was stunned. I said, 'What did I do? I was just sitting in my seat minding my own business before John asked me to have a word with the steward.' The captain wasn't bothered. He said John would have to get off, so would I and so would Mick, who had been drinking coffee at the airport bar. John Carroll from my management team came up to plead our case but he was told he'd be thrown off as well if he didn't keep quiet.

We were in business class and it was clear some of the passengers must have objected to all of us. The irony was that Air Malta was actually supporting the tournament that I had just won. Now they were telling us to get off the plane and go back to the airport. I was desperate for them to change their mind because it had been a long week and I just wanted to get home. I told them what a beautiful country Malta was, how hospitable they'd been and how much we were looking forward to coming back. I tried everything to appease them but they didn't budge. There was no more arguing to be done. We just had to leave.

They called out a member of airport security and he escorted us off the plane and took us to a bus to transfer us back to the terminal. We pleaded with him as well and he went back on to the plane to ask the captain if he'd change his mind, not least because of the time it would take to get our bags off, but he didn't and our fate was sealed. The flight was therefore delayed by something like two hours while all this was going on. Everyone on the plane must have been thoroughly fed up.

We took a taxi back to the hotel because the next flight wasn't until four in the afternoon. When we got back to the airport we were basically given a security escort. I said to John, 'Don't go to the bar!' Wisely, we all had coffees. We got on the plane, took off and slept on the flight. As we were landing at Heathrow, we started joking that there'd be police waiting for us and about what our other halves would make of it all. We had no idea of what was about to happen. We got off the flight and there were three photographers and the airport PR guy waiting for us. A cameraman started flashing away and the people behind us must have thought, 'These snooker players must get this all the time.' It was like we were film stars. You'd see it if David Beckham got off a flight and had to do that long walk through the airport. I can't say I enjoyed it.

Every few steps we took they ran in front of us, taking yet more pictures. It felt like we'd been set up but we'd been naive about the impact a story like this would have. The British and Irish papers were tipped off by someone in Malta and then the whole thing snowballed out of control. The next day it seemed to be the only thing anyone was talking about. That became apparent when Mick phoned me up and asked if I'd seen the papers. I was on every front page looking sheepish and then on the back page there was me with the trophy.

The whole thing upset me a lot at the time. I've always tried to be a professional, as has John, and yet there we were, plastered – some thought literally – across the newspapers for being drunk and out of control on a flight. I'm sure people must have thought the worst of us. When you hear about something like that it's tempting to think it's just a bunch of rich, spoilt sportsmen, arrogantly thinking they can behave however they want without any consequences. I didn't want people to think that about me and was disappointed by some of the coverage, which seemed way over the top compared to what had actually happened.

I was worried as well what effect it would have on my family but, once I explained to them the true story, they were fine about it. Eamon Dunphy rang me the next day. He'd been reading all the stuff in the papers and he said, 'The best thing to do is not to hide from it. If any radio stations or newspapers ring you up and ask for an interview, do it. Come clean and tell them what happened. If you don't do that then it looks like you've got something to hide.' So I went on Gerry Ryan's show on RTE and with Matt Cooper on Today FM and all the other big shows. I said I was sorry if I'd embarrassed anyone but explained what happened and it all went away pretty quickly. I'd managed to make a joke of it and ultimately most people seemed to think it was pretty funny, not least because I wasn't a snooker player you would expect to be caught up in something like that. It was the end of my Mary Poppins image.

The week after all this happened I went to the Liverpool v Manchester United match in the FA Cup at Anfield and flew into Liverpool Airport. It was seven in the morning but the whole flight was drinking and singing. It was a really raucous atmosphere. They were all taking the piss out of me, telling me, 'Now, no drinking today, Ken. You don't want to get thrown off another flight.' I didn't mind because it was good natured. What could you say? But the whole plane seemed to be drunk and it was total mayhem. Had they been on the plane back from Malta then they all would have been ordered off. It felt like a bit of an injustice when you compared their behaviour with ours.

I'm not trying to present an idealised version of events but it's important to clarify how it all unfolded. John was drunk – he would be the first to admit that. I can understand it if other passengers were wary of him but he wasn't behaving in a loutish or belligerent way at all. He would not have posed any danger to anyone. I wasn't drunk and neither was Mick. Our crime was merely standing up for our friend. I think the fact we were snooker players – or recognisable figures – counted against us. The captain of that flight seemed to want to make an example of us.

I still occasionally get people mentioning it but it hasn't followed me round in the long term or done any real damage to my reputation. Maybe people even saw me in a different light. John pretty much quit drinking after it happened – his wife, Denise, hadn't been too impressed – and went on to win the world title the following year, so it may even have done him some sort of favour.

It's fair to say, though, that when I opened the newspapers the morning after our aeroplane drama it felt like one of the lowest moments of my career.

CHAPTER FOURTEEN

SIX APPEAL

18 December 2009

I'm in Killarney where Mark Davis has just beaten Mark Williams to win the first ever Six Reds World Championship. This event is of particular significance for me because I helped to organise it.

Six reds snooker is exactly as it sounds: the same game with nine fewer reds. It's designed to be faster and satisfy television audiences who find the traditional game a bit slow and boring. Kids who aren't interested in the 15-red game might prefer the shorter version. A typical frame can be over in seven or eight minutes so it's quicker than the established format and has been successful in attracting new audiences to snooker in Asia, where there have been two big international events in Bangkok in the last couple of years.

In the summer of 2009 I sat down with Connie O'Sullivan, Ray Power, David Joyce and Andrew Spillane to discuss putting on a big tournament in Killarney. There had been a World Series event, organised by John Higgins and his manager, at the INEC Arena here a few weeks earlier and it had done well. My idea was to have a big Irish Open tournament but having just played in the successful six reds competition in Bangkok, I thought we should go down that route because it would be something different for an Irish audience. We wondered if we could get enough players to justify calling it a World Championship but the other side of the coin was that if we did give it that name, more players would be likely to enter.

We had to build the tournament from scratch and we probably could have done with a few extra months. Having been a player, I hadn't realised the amount of work that goes into getting an event off the ground. Players are used to just turning up and playing but there's a huge effort behind the scenes that we never see to get to that point. My role was to sell it to the players and get as many of them to enter as possible, particularly the big names.

Snooker has been through the wars and has struggled to attract attention outside the majors such as the World and UK Championships and the Wembley Masters. As sponsors have come and gone and tournaments have been moved around different venues, the events have lost their identity and are therefore no longer as special as they once were. That's where six reds could play a part because it's a new concept and a bit of a novelty. Cricket has brought in Twenty/20 for those who don't enjoy Test matches and there's no reason why snooker shouldn't aim to do similarly. We have a great sport but for various reasons, many people who used to follow it no longer do.

Here in Killarney, it's been a relaxed atmosphere. We have a huge playing area divided up into 13 tables, with one configured for TV coverage. It's all open and that means the public can roam around from table to table and watch whichever matches they want. The tournament has gone well for a first effort. We got Eurosport to cover the last two days live and 888sport.com came in as sponsor. The players, both professionals and amateurs, seem happy and it's been an enjoyable experience. That said, there are things we could have done better. I was disappointed with the crowds. We need to promote the event better. You learn how to improve an event like this from actually doing it and we'll take suggestions on board. The main thing was that we actually got the tournament on, which in itself was no mean feat. We can make a few little tweaks going forward but this wasn't a bad start.

The biggest disappointment for me was the attitude of some of the players who entered and then pulled out before the tournament began, which complicated things because the first stage was played in groups, where the top stars were seeded. It meant a lot of extra work changing players round and bringing in reserves. I was delighted that Stephen Hendry, John Higgins and Mark Williams were among the players who came over, because they are all world champions and recognised as all-time greats. They added the prestige you need if you call your tournament a World Championship. We had more than 30 other professionals play here too and I'm grateful to them for supporting the event. We needed big names to make it attractive to TV and sponsors. However, Shaun Murphy let us down. His manager phoned me the day before we were due to start and said he didn't think the prize money – €35,000 – was high enough and that Shaun wouldn't be playing. The first prize was €10,000. If that isn't enough for Shaun for just four days' work in a new tournament then he's a lot better off than I thought. Mark Allen said he had a new cue and wanted to practise with it. Peter Ebdon said he had a back injury.

It's fair enough not to enter or even to withdraw in good time, but not to pull out at the last minute when it's been advertised that you're in the tournament. It made things awkward for us. It was bloody hard work getting this on but snooker players can be prima donnas, thinking they are a lot bigger than they actually are. They don't always appreciate the people working hard behind the scenes to provide them with a living. So many players say – and I'd agree with them – that we haven't had enough tournaments. This was a new one with decent money available and yet still it wasn't good enough for certain players.

What did please me, though, was the turnout by amateur players from all around the world. So many of them came up to me to say how much they enjoyed it and that they would never have ordinarily got the chance to play top stars. My friend Shea Brereton, who used to own one of the oldest snooker clubs in Ireland, the Home of Billiards, came down with me on the train. Shea lives and breathes snooker. He just loves it. He was drawn in Hendry's group and we were all kidding him on that Stephen was shaking in his boots. Shea loved the week and he was typical of the amateurs who came to play and have already told me they'll be back next time if we can get it on again.

In terms of the way the arena was laid out, the tournament reminded me of the 1991 World Masters, which was played in Birmingham and promoted by Barry Hearn. That also featured a large hall with a number of tables and was a fun event, although it proved too costly to hold again.

This week Barry was confirmed as chairman of the World Professional Billiards and Snooker Association, the governing body of the professional game, after the previous incumbent, Sir Rodney Walker, was voted out. Barry has a long history in snooker, having managed Steve Davis since the 1970s and promoted many events over the years, most prominently the Premier League. If he does half as well running snooker as he has done running the Professional Darts Corporation then the sport is set for good times again. The darts lads play in huge arenas in front of thousands of spectators and have seen their earnings increase dramatically. Barry is a great salesman and his enthusiasm is infectious. He is brilliant at identifying a niche market and then exploiting it, giving the people what they want even if they didn't realise they wanted it.

Put it this way: snooker under Barry Hearn can't be any worse than it was with the previous lot. Some of the guys on the board were living in dreamland as far as I was concerned. They were making statements to the effect that the game was better off than before they were elected and that there was money in the bank and so on. The fact is, we started this season with only six ranking events, which was two fewer than last year and far too few for a sport as popular on television as snooker. I'm afraid the image of snooker is that it's on the wane and it's true that it has fallen away since I turned professional.

I'm glad Walker and other board members were voted off because they were living in a fantasy world. They didn't have the commitment required to turn things round and seemed to see it as easy money for themselves. Barry Hearn isn't in it just to make money, because he's making loads from darts. Barry loves snooker and is on record as saying he feels he owes the game for the opportunities it's given him. I think he's the right man to lead us out of the mire.

I'm a traditionalist at heart and I hope he doesn't change the big tournaments but I'm all for different concepts and formats as well, such as six reds or doubles or a World Cup. Anything that brings additional interest to the game has to be embraced. We're in the situation now where we can't be choosy or turn our noses up at new ideas. I realise people may be worried about changes but things can't simply stay as they are. People need to open their eyes and stop living in the past.

CHAPTER FIFTEEN

THE ONE THAT GOT AWAY

B ecoming world champion changed my life but it also made me re-evaluate my goals. My first ambition had been to turn professional, then to win a title and then to capture the World Championship. After reaching this pinnacle my immediate objective was to continue the push for success and not to take my foot off the pedal because I knew there would be even more expectation on my shoulders and I didn't want to be seen as some kind of one hit wonder.

But being world champion carries with it a great many responsibilities and these mean more demands on your time, to the extent that your normal practice regime is seriously affected. Suddenly you are being phoned up to make personal appearances, undertake exhibitions and are invited on to all sorts of television programmes, such as *A Question of Sport* and various chat shows. I threw myself into this because I knew I might never get the chance again, plus it was important to promote snooker as its world champion.

I was determined to enjoy my year as Crucible king after all the work I'd put in to achieve my dream and there was no better feeling than being introduced into arenas as the reigning world champion. The applause and acclaim, the feeling of pride, puts a spring in your step before you've struck a ball on the table and is a constant reminder of what you've achieved. However, it does also put you under a bit of pressure. For your opponent, to beat the world champion is a great scalp and so you do feel as if you're the one being hunted in every tournament.

It's hard to win any event but with this additional pressure, plus the fact that I didn't have as much time to concentrate on my game, it wasn't that surprising looking back that my season as champion was a little disappointing. I won a title in Malta and lost three close ranking tournament semi-finals but of course I wanted to bolster my trophy cabinet considerably off the back of winning the biggest prize of all.

It was an ultra-competitive time. Stephen Hendry might have lost his world title but he was still the man to beat. John Higgins had emerged as his closest challenger for top spot and was playing the best snooker of anyone that season. Ronnie O'Sullivan and Mark Williams were winning titles and there were the likes of Peter Ebdon, John Parrott, Alan McManus and Nigel Bond all up there and capable of beating anybody on their day.

It was a weird feeling in a way to walk back into the

Crucible Theatre for the 1998 World Championship. Once again the focus of attention was on me and I felt the memories of the previous year come flooding back. The one thing I was desperate to avoid was a first-day exit. In snooker there is something known as the 'Crucible curse' that afflicts first-time champions. Since the tournament moved to Sheffield in 1977 no first-time winner has made a successful defence of the title. Joe Johnson got the closest by losing 18-14 to Steve Davis in the 1987 final and, 11 years on, I would get almost as close by reaching the final again.

It was a huge relief just to get past Lee Walker on that first Saturday. I felt nervous but also excited and inspired when I walked back into the arena that morning to experience the unique Crucible atmosphere again. I started well, winning the first three frames and eventually ending the opening session 6-3 up. I went back to the hotel, relaxed, then headed back for the final session in the evening hoping to kill the match off as quickly as possible. As it transpired it turned into something of a scramble for the winning line.

I lost two tight frames but still went to the interval 8-5 up after making a 134 break, my second century of the match. I looked likely to win comfortably at that point but Lee came back with three frames on the spin and it was suddenly 8-8 and anybody's match. I knew I had to dig deep and try to apply the same mindset as I had the previous year. I controlled the 17th frame and then won a much closer one to finally get myself into the second round. I was hugely relieved. To go from the elation of my final victory over Hendry to the misery of a first-day defeat would have been a horrible feeling. It was close but my attempt to beat the famous curse was off and running.

With this nervous first-round match out of the way I started to play well. I beat Stephen Lee 13-8 in the second round and Matthew Stevens, who was fast emerging as one to watch, 13-10 in the quarter-finals. In the semis I went from 6-2 up against Mark Williams to trail 13-11 going into the final session, but my experience told and I held it together to reach the final again.

It was unbelievable, really. I'd dreamed of appearing in a world final and now here I was in my second in as many years. I knew it would be tough, though. I was up against John Higgins, a player I knew to possess a rock-solid temperament as well as a game as good as anyone's. John went 6-1 up. I came back to 6-5 but was 10-6 down overnight. I still believed I could win the match and closed to trail only 13-11 before he beat me 18-12. I was disappointed to lose but proud that I had reached another final and come closer than anyone other than Johnson to defending the title in my first season as champion.

The next few years brought me a fair amount of success as well as a few near-misses. In early 2001 I won the Welsh Open for a second time, beating Paul Hunter 9-2 in the final in Cardiff. I was playing really well and went to the next ranking tournament, the Thailand Masters, full of confidence and stormed through the field, hammering Stephen Hendry 9-3 in the final. I felt great, as if I'd hit a real purple patch, and wanted to keep it going right up to the Crucible.

The signs were good. I reached the final of the next event as well, the Scottish Open in Aberdeen, and was on course to join Hendry, Steve Davis and Ray Reardon as the only players to win three ranking titles in a row. I very nearly did it, too, but lost a lengthy and frankly pretty dull final 9-7 to the grinding Peter Ebdon. My bid for a second world title ended at the quarter-final stage a few weeks later with defeat to Higgins but I still felt I was playing some of my best stuff and that more titles could follow.

Prior to this I'd reached the Masters final at Wembley Conference Centre two years running, losing 10-8 to John Higgins in 1999 and by the same score to Matthew Stevens a year later. That final was memorable for me missing the last black of a 147, about which I've already told you.

I was also a finalist in another of snooker's most prestigious events, the UK Championship, two years in succession. In 2001 Ronnie O'Sullivan obliterated me 10-1 in about as good a performance as you could witness. He was simply awesome. Winning one frame felt like an achievement to me. A year later it was a completely different story. I was through to the final against Mark Williams, who was playing some of his best ever snooker, and he beat me 10-9 in the decider, a defeat I found really hard to take. Little did I know it would foreshadow one of my best tournaments but also biggest disappointments just a few months later.

When people look back at the 2003 World Championship they probably remember my matches more than those of the eventual champion. I ended up playing more frames in that championship than any player has before or since. For the record it was 132 out of a possible 137, and I still don't know how I made it to the final night without keeling over. As it was, I came agonisingly close to pulling off what would have been a fairytale victory.

The pattern for the 2003 tournament was set in the first round when I cleared up the six colours to pip the emerging Shaun Murphy 10-9 on the final black. That proved to be a foretaste of what the rest of the tournament would be like.

In the second round I played Graeme Dott. He had always been tough to beat but was starting to really improve at around this time. A year later he was in the final himself and in 2006 he won the title. He made by far the better start in our match, opening a 7-2 lead before I scraped home 13-12. It was another match that got the heart rate racing beyond belief. I'd managed to steady the ship by pulling back to within two frames at 9-7 down going into the final session and then went 12-10 ahead but Graeme, as he always does, fought hard and I didn't get much of a look-in during the next two frames.

I've played so many deciders in my career and you are basically just hoping to get some sort of chance. It was another close frame but I managed to win it on the colours and fall into the quarter-finals. It didn't get any easier. I was up against John Higgins, always one of the favourites to win the title. You never really know how any match is going to pan out but nobody – myself included – would have expected me to open a 10-0 lead.

I remember leaving the Crucible after the first session when I was 8-0 up. I had to wait for a courtesy car back to the hotel and out came John, cue in hand, just staring at the floor. He looked a completely broken man. All the life had been knocked out of him and it looked like he'd already given up.

I came out for the second session and quickly won the first two frames. It was surreal in a way. Here I was, in the biggest tournament of the year against one of the best players in the world, and everything was going right. It was like dream snooker. I played out of my skin in the early part of the match and after two deciders it looked certain that I would win easily. An unprecedented 13-0 whitewash wasn't out of the question. It didn't happen, though: John won the next seven frames and I was suddenly bang under pressure.

I had wanted to win with a session to spare to give myself more time to prepare for the semi-finals but it proved to be the wrong mindset. The match was far from over as John hadn't given up at all. He made a century to win his first frame and then started to knock everything in. He won all the remaining frames of the middle session, the last three of which were all close and a reminder to me that I was still involved in a match.

It was weird because if you'd had said to me before the start of play that I would be 10-6 up going into the final session I'd have been delighted, but to be 10-6 up having led 10-0 was a different ball game entirely. I was really nervous going into the final session, even though I was four frames ahead. I was thinking that if I lost from 10-0 up it would be an historic defeat. I said at the time it would have been the biggest collapse since Wall Street in the 1920s. It would have been an utter disaster, the sort of defeat you might never get over. We've all lost from a few in front in our time but that would have taken a lifetime – maybe several lifetimes – to get over.

It proved, too, that the Crucible can be the best place in the world to be when you're playing well, but the loneliest when you find yourself completely shut out and staring down the barrel of a humiliating defeat, one that may even come to define your whole career. It happened to Jimmy White at the hands of Stephen Hendry when he was coasting to the title in 1992, leading 14-8 and then failing to win another frame. So the nerves were really flying around my body and they weren't helped when John won the first frame of the session to close to 10-7.

John isn't a player you'd ever choose to play in the World Championship. He's so determined and such a good all-round competitor that when it's him coming back at you the doubts start to fester. As he got closer to me he'd have started to fancy the job. His body language for the final session was the exact reverse of the dejected figure who had stood outside the Crucible after the first eight frames. He was up for this now and it would be a test of my temperament and coolness under gathering pressure.

The next frame was massive. I potted a great pink to get on the black and then potted that as well to lead 11-7, and that restored a bit of breathing space and halted John's momentum. After that I felt a lot better inside and went on to win 13-8. Even though that scoreline seems reasonably comfortable when written down it was anything but. It further depleted my already well used reserves of mental energy and I still had five days to go – a possible 68 frames – if I was going to become world champion for the second time.

Paul Hunter was my opponent in the semi-finals. Paul had emerged in the previous few years as not only an outstanding talent but also a crowd favourite. His image as a man of the people in the Jimmy White mould was sealed by an innocent remark he made to the press after pulling back from 6-2 down to beat Fergal O'Brien 10-9 in the final of the 2001 Wembley Masters. Asked why there had been such a turnaround in fortunes, he revealed that he had spent the break between sessions in his hotel room with his gorgeous girlfriend, Lindsey, and that they had 'put Plan B into operation'. There was nothing calculated about this revelation but Paul ended up on the front page of some newspapers and it cemented his status as a fans' favourite.

He'd won the Masters again in 2002 and beat me in the Welsh Open final at around the same time. Paul was clearly a potential world champion and he got off to a good start in our semi-final, winning the first session 6-2, leading 11-5 after the second and holding a 15-9 advantage heading into the final afternoon, which left him only two frames from the final.

I'd played well during the tournament but felt that my great run was finally over. I didn't feel like my game was there in the early stages of the match and Paul dominated proceedings to such an extent that he looked the only winner. At 15-9 down I just decided to play each frame and try to keep the match going as long as I could. It's an old cliché but you really do have to take it one frame at a time in that situation.

I made two good breaks, a 73 and a 93, to close to 15-11 and then I won a black ball frame and noticed that Paul was getting increasingly nervous. He'd missed the yellow to lead 16-11 and it was the first sign that he was feeling anxious. It had been hard for him, coming out so far in front with everyone around him no doubt already making preparations for the final while he knew, as I had against Higgins, that the match wasn't over and that it would be a crushing blow to lose from such a commanding position.

It was unbelievably tense. I won another close frame and so went to the interval having won the first four frames and now trailing only 15-13. You could sense that the audience knew this was now up for grabs. I'm sure Paul felt that as well and I certainly felt I had a chance. He started missing, I had a bit of luck and I won another frame to make it just 15-14. I just tried to pile the pressure on him. I knew what happened in that scenario: your arms start to wobble, your legs start to shake and you can't feel your cue properly. You can sense that in your opponent and I could see Paul was becoming more anxious with every frame I won.

He eventually ended this run by winning the 30th frame to lead 16-14 and I wondered if my chance had gone. But then I fluked a blue to make it 16-15, which was obviously a major blow to Paul. After that I won the last two frames pretty easily to clinch an improbable 17-16 victory and take my place in the final.

It was incredible. I felt elated, as if I'd won the title. It was the best comeback of my career and to do it at the Crucible against a world-class player made it all the more amazing. I suppose the difference in the end could have been experience that afternoon. I'd been there before whereas it was Paul's first Crucible semi-final. Paul was so gracious afterwards that it was one of the few times that I actually felt sorry for an opponent who'd lost. Paul was such a lovely lad and it would have meant so much for him to be in a world final. Tragic circumstances meant he would never get his chance again. That's the only thing now about that match that detracts from the achievement for me, the fact that Paul's life was cut so horribly short, dying of a rare cancer at 27. I wish in a way the match had happened against someone else.

The final was against Mark Williams, who had coasted into the final losing only 19 frames compared to my 45. Mark was playing superbly at the time. He was the world no.1, he'd already won the UK Championship and the Masters that season and was looking to land the world title to join Steve Davis and Stephen Hendry as the only players to have won snooker's 'big three' titles in a single campaign.

I was exhausted but determined to put in one last great effort. However, the first day of the final turned into a nightmare for me. Mark won the first session 7-1 and was leading 10-2 at one stage before I won three of the last four frames of the evening session to trail 11-5 overnight. I suppose by now everyone was expecting a comeback from me and it duly occurred. I knew I could have been even further behind going into the second day and refused to believe the final was over. I'd felt the effects of the Hunter match in the early part of the final and I felt like my brains were scrambled, added to which I was playing the best player in the world at that time.

But on the final day I decided I'd come this far and it was time to fight for the title. I came out and won the first six frames to level at 11-11 and after Mark won the next, I made my second century of the afternoon to make it 12-12 going into the final session. It felt like the battle of all battles and I fancied going on to win. I'd got to him and he started to feel the pressure, just as Paul had in the previous round. Mark, however, had won the title in 2000 after coming back against Matthew Stevens, so he had had experience of how to cope in the heat of the Crucible.

I'm sure he was glad when the break came. It gave him a chance to get his head together while I would have liked to have stayed out there. We traded frames in the evening, reaching the last interval of the championship level at 14-14. Mark then went a couple ahead but I pulled it back to 16-16, making a third century in the process. Eventually the fight proved to be in vain. Mark won the last two frames fairly easily and was the winner 18-16. The fairytale ending refused to come. It was over and I had lost. The record books will show that he was the winner, not me, regardless of the tournament I'd had.

Losing that final is still the biggest disappointment of my career. I took that harder than any match I'd lost. I battled as well as anyone ever has but still came away without the trophy. All the compliments and accolades I received for my performance, well meant though they were by players, fans and pundits, could not make up for finishing runner-up. It had felt like I was destined to win it but sport doesn't work like that. It's not like a film or TV show. I'm sure the party that night would have eclipsed the one we'd had in 1997 if I'd done it but it wasn't to be.

It took a long time for me to get over not only losing, but losing to Mark. We weren't friends by any means and had had a run-in at the UK Championship a few months earlier. Before the final, he came to my dressing room and suggested we split the prize fund, so that whoever won we'd get the same amount. I refused and he wasn't happy. To me, it was short-changing the public because if they'd found out what we'd agreed, they'd think we didn't care which one of us won as we'd be getting an identical cheque. To me, that was just wrong. I'm aware it has happened before and I'm not for a minute suggesting Mark wasn't trying to win but I couldn't be any part of something like that. He got the needle – and beat me 10-9 – and we hadn't really patched things up by the time of our Crucible final, so to lose to him made it even worse.

I had to swallow the defeat but it was the end of the season so I had a lot of time to sulk about it. You replay certain shots in your mind or ask yourself why you couldn't have done this differently, played the right shot there, but you know it's all pointless. I couldn't change anything that had happened. There are those who say I should have won a second world title that year. Maybe they are right but it's a lot easier said than done. If anything it brought home just what an achievement it had been to win it in 1997 because it proved how hard becoming world champion really was.

Some people say that I was the true world champion that year but I don't see it like that. Mark won it fair and square and deserved the title. He showed what a great player he was by holding on after my latest comeback.

But in time, despite my disappointment at getting so close and then just coming up short, I became proud of myself for the effort I put in over those 17 days. I couldn't have done any more. It really was the one that got away.

CHAPTER SIXTEEN

SLOW PROGRESS

Prestatyn, 5 February 2010

Since Shanghai I've failed to qualify for the final stages of another ranking tournament but this is not the disaster that it sounds. First, there were only three events. Secondly, I won my first match in each before going down in the final qualifying round to players who belong in the top 16.

Jamie Cope beat me in the UK Championship. He's a very dangerous young player, attacking and deadly at long potting, who has already been in a couple of ranking tournament finals. I was 3-0 up and he needed a snooker in the fourth frame. He got it, cleared up and I went to the interval 3-1 ahead rather than 4-0. That threw Jamie a lifeline and inspired him. It helped him find his game and he went on to beat me 9-6. I felt I should have won but that one frame turned the whole match.

That can happen anywhere. It's happened to me before and will happen again. What was significant was that the frame came before the interval. There aren't dressing rooms in Prestatyn, just a big players' room. When you come off for the mid-session break you notice where your opponent is sitting and find a seat as far away from him as possible. I spent the 15-minute break cursing myself for letting the frame slip by, because a 4-0 lead would have been considerable as I had played well and felt my confidence growing. Meanwhile, Jamie could sit there geeing himself up for the re-start and telling himself he still had every chance of getting back into the match.

Intervals often do this. They help turn matches because they sow seeds of hope for one player and uncertainty for the other. It's no overstatement to say that the whole course of snooker history would be different were it not for intervals. Matches have swung round as a result of play having to stop, allowing one player to regroup and the other to contemplate defeat when victory was looking likely. It can be horrible to be sat in a dressing room, alone with your thoughts. Sometimes the intervals can seem like an eternity whereas sometimes you're glad of the break as it offers a respite if things are going badly for you. It illustrates how important psychology is in snooker when a period when you aren't playing ultimately has a bearing on the result.

I still went to the UK Championship as a BBC pundit but I couldn't help thinking what might have been. My defeat to Jamie was the first real setback of what I felt had been a good season up to that point. I had some momentum and wanted to keep it going. Unfortunately I was unable to do that in the next two qualifiers.

Graeme Dott beat me in the Welsh Open and then again today in the China Open. It wasn't the best of draws bearing in mind it's only a few years since he and I were challenging for the world no.1 position. Graeme has had his problems, including depression, but he won the world title in 2006 and is such a tough campaigner. His form seems to have returned and I was surprised at how well he played against me in the Prestatyn environment, where I would have expected him to struggle after several years in the top 16.

Jamie and Graeme are two of the toughest players I could have drawn but I'm not complaining, because it's always going to be hard in the qualifying jungle. The key thing is that I haven't lost a first-round match. That's important for the rankings because you only get half points if you lose your initial match. Last season I lost five first-rounders and that cost me dearly. That's why I ended up 44th in the list and contemplating retirement.

So although I haven't maintained what was an encouraging start to the season, at least I have still won matches and am not dropping back in the rankings, even if I'm not making huge strides up the list. If I qualify for the final stages of the World Championship I'll be certain to return to the top 32, which means I will have one fewer qualifying match per event to play next year. Moving back up was my aim at the start of the season and it's what I've managed to do, so I have to take those positives.

That doesn't mean I've fallen in love with Prestatyn. Far

LIFE IN THE FRAME

from it. Nobody enjoys coming here because of the pressure and the fine line between winning and going into the final stages of a tournament and losing and having to watch it on the TV. Next season the qualifiers are apparently moving to Sheffield. I'm all for that because I think it's a better set-up there but the tension will be the same. What it means to everyone will be the same.

Perhaps the worst thing about the slump I endured was that I didn't know whether that was me finished at the age of 40 or whether it was just a blip, that my form had gone walkabout and would return. I was at a career crossroads for that reason and this season has been one of discovery: do I still have what it takes or not?

I've proved to myself that I can still win matches and this is the start of what I hope is a journey back to the top 16. I realise time is against me but the encouraging results I've had this year sure beats sliding down the rankings.

CHAPTER SEVENTEEN

PLAYERS AND ME

The snooker circuit is by and large a friendly place. We are fierce rivals on the table but most players get on backstage. You spend so much time travelling with these guys and sitting around at tournament venues that it's inevitable relationships form. It's not the case with every player, though. In any workplace you will meet people you gel with and those you don't. Also, it could be argued that it's a disadvantage if you like someone. I certainly find it hard playing close friends. Perhaps it takes away a little bit of your competitive instinct.

In this chapter I have picked out some of the best known players I've played against as a professional. On a personal level I may get on with some better than others, but they are all fascinating characters in their own right and have all contributed to snooker being such a popular sport for television audiences around the world.

Steve Davis

When I was 14, I won a junior club tournament and together with the other finalist won a trip to the Crucible Theatre in Sheffield. It was only two years after I'd watched Alex Higgins win the title on the TV and I couldn't have been more excited to be going there for the first time. We saw Steve play his first-round match against Neal Foulds, who he beat 10-8. It was a great experience to be at the Crucible, although it was so warm in the arena that I fell asleep! I wasn't used to the heat and we were sat there for hours.

Seven years later I qualified for the first time and drew Steve in the first round. The match was to be played on the same table where I'd watched him beat Neal Foulds. I went out into the arena, saw my name up in lights next to Steve's and I just couldn't believe it. It didn't seem real somehow because it hadn't been that long since I'd been up in the audience and now here I was, actually playing him. I was totally distracted by all my feelings of nostalgia and by Steve's record of success at the Crucible, and before I knew what was happening he was 4-0 up within about an hour. He must have been thinking it would be an easy win against this fresh-faced kid who was completely naive and not used to the environment. I got my head together at the interval and came out to win four of the remaining five frames of the session, to trail just 5-4. I later got it to 8-8 and although he won 10-8, I'd put up a tough fight and made him work for the win. I'd got over my earlier feelings of awe and came out of the match proud of myself and feeling I'd learned loads.

Steve has always been a terrific match-player. Even now, in his fifties, he's tough to beat. In the second round of the 2010 World Championship he beat John Higgins, the defending champion, 13-11, which was an incredible result, one of the all-time shocks. Steve became the first fifty-something Crucible quarter-finalist for 27 years and there wasn't anyone in the game who wasn't made up for him because we all know how much he loves the game. That's one of the reasons he is still managing to get results long after he should, theoretically, have slid so far down the rankings that he'd no longer be on the circuit.

As a character Steve has his own idiosyncrasies. He can act a little strangely at times and be quite aloof. He'll talk to you one minute and blank you the next. But as a player he is the master. You can learn so much about safety and the tactical side of the game by playing him or watching him, observing the shots that he plays that nobody else would think of. When I played him back in 1991 it felt like an education.

He can also be a bit bloody-minded. I played him in the Irish Masters in 1992 and it was 4-4 and into a deciding frame. There's a rule in snooker that had just come in that if you fail to make contact with a ball three successive times when you're not snookered, you lose the frame. Steve missed twice and in that situation the last thing you would normally do is play the same shot again, particularly if it would cost you not just the frame but the match as well. Well, he did play it the same way and he missed again. The crowd didn't understand what was happening when the referee said, 'Foul and a miss, frame and match Ken Doherty.' It was the first time a televised frame, let alone a match, had finished like that. I went into Steve's dressing room afterwards to commiserate with him. It wasn't a nice way to win, although deep down I was obviously delighted to have beaten him, but he was very nice about it, admitting it was his own fault. Back at the hotel that night he was on the practice table playing exactly the same shot over and over again. I suppose it shows how obsessed he is, a trait in great champions from any sport.

He still has an aura even now. We do exhibitions around Ireland and he seems to love snooker as much as ever. The evenings usually end with a trick-shot routine from Steve, which might not start until something like 11pm but instead of doing two or three shots over 20 minutes he always wants to get up and do 45 minutes, because he loves telling his stories and making people laugh. Everyone is waiting to go home but he'll be up there, entertaining all and sundry. His image in the 1980s was of someone completely boring but anyone who knows Steve knows that simply isn't true. He has a nice, dry wit and can be hilarious. He plays up to the 'interesting' tag that *Spitting Image* gave him and has developed into one of the circuit's most popular players.

I play a lot of poker now, as do many snooker players, and it was Steve who got us all into that. I came to the UK Championship a few years ago and Steve was on his laptop in the press room. He was sat there for hours. I asked him what he was doing and he said he was playing poker online against various people around the world. I couldn't get my head around it at first. It seemed like a strange way to spend time. Yet Steve started a revolution because now almost everyone in snooker seems to play poker and it's almost as if we all felt that if Steve was doing something, it was worth us doing it as well. He's become a sort of figurehead in that respect, someone we all look up to, someone we all follow.

What Steve has also done is prove that you can have a snooker career into your forties and fifties, something that gives me encouragement. It's funny because I never supported him when he was a player in the 1980s as he usually beat Alex Higgins, my personal hero, but I really look up to him now. He's won so much in his career that he could have retired gracefully but it's a testament to how much he loves the game that he's carried on. It's not just playing Steve enjoys but being around the tournaments, working for the BBC and experiencing the rush you get just being involved in a big event, and I can relate to that.

It's weird that I've ended up next to Steve on the BBC sofa, bearing in mind how excited I was to see him play at the Crucible all those years ago, and then to play him myself. He's good to work with because he's so funny and although I don't always agree with his analysis, I respect his opinions. We tend to talk about poker the minute the camera is off us, and we've built a good rapport. If I can keep playing to the standard Steve has maintained as he's got older then I'll be more than happy.

Mark Williams

Mark is a tremendous player and has twice won the World Championship, UK Championship and Wembley Masters as well as being world no.1, but he isn't someone I've ever really got on with.

We didn't get off to the best of starts because I upset him with something I said after Stephen Hendry beat me in the semi-finals of the 1998 Masters. Stephen was through to play Mark in the final and I said in the press conference that I thought if Hendry played like he had against me then he would win, due to how well he was playing and the fact he'd already won the title six times. (As it transpired, he lost 10-9 to Williams on a re-spotted black.) I wasn't being disrespectful to Mark, I was just giving my honest opinion, but it apparently irked him and we never really saw eye-to-eye after that.

He's the sort of person who does his own thing rather than mixing with everyone else. He doesn't make much of an effort when he's on television and usually goes around tournaments in a tracksuit when he's not playing. That's up to him, but it isn't my definition of what a professional is. I always thought players should look a certain way, act a certain way and treat other people a certain way but he doesn't fall into that category.

Don't get me wrong, he's one of the best players I've ever come up against. He beat me in two finals I will never forget – the 2002 UK Championship, which went to a deciding frame, and the 2003 World Championship, when he came through 18-16. They were great struggles and I salute him for the way he played in both finals but the defeats were harder to take because I lost to someone I'm not friends with. I suppose we have a personality clash because we're different sorts of people. He's not someone I particularly look to spend time with at a tournament and I'm sure he feels the same about me. There's no nastiness between us but there's definitely an edge when we play.

Stephen Hendry

I first met Stephen in 1984 at Prestatyn for the Home Internationals, a big annual amateur team event, where he was representing Scotland and I was playing for Ireland. Even then, it was clear he was going to be a star – and he knew it. He'd walk around with his nose up in the air, not talking to anyone. He was so cocky it was unbelievable. He understood exactly where he was going and what he was going to achieve in the game. He looked the business and he played sublime snooker even then but he was aloof and he stayed like that to an extent. He wanted to separate himself from everyone else and develop an aura. It's a great thing to have and it's the way you've got to be to get to the top, but it means isolating yourself from everyone else and that's not something that comes easily to most of us.

Even now, you can know people like Hendry and Davis but not really know them. They're the sort of people who keep a lot inside. I don't really know much about Stephen's life or what he does outside snooker but we have had some laughs as well on the circuit. He's good company but he is also single-minded and didn't come into snooker to make friends. Not everyone would like that but in a way I wish I'd been more like him.

Stephen is the best player I've ever played against. At his

best, he was awesome, better even than Ronnie O'Sullivan. His long potting and break-building were out of this world and his safety game, when he used it, was strong as well. Unlike Ronnie, you knew Stephen would not go to pieces psychologically. He had such inner strength and belief in his own abilities. The only way I could beat him was by breaking him down, playing good match snooker and trying to frustrate him. It felt like you had to hide the cue ball in your pocket to keep him out and stop him scoring. Just when you thought you had him in trouble on the bottom cushion he would pull out a pot from nowhere and make a frame-winning break.

When I played him in the 1994 UK Championship final, he beat me 10-5 and made seven centuries, which is still a record. It must be the best anyone has ever played. He led 6-5 and I was at the table in the next frame. I potted a black on 24, went into the pack and a red dropped into the middle pocket. Stephen got in and made another century, his sixth in the seven frames he'd won. We went off for the interval and my pal Eamon Dunphy, who was over with me, burst into my dressing room. I was sat sulking in my chair and Eamon was raging. He was shouting, 'Don't worry about that frame, he's fucking gone! You have him by the bollocks!' This was at Preston Guild Hall, where the walls between the dressing rooms were as thin as cardboard. I was telling him to keep it down but he kept on. 'I hope he hears me! I hope he hears me!' So we went out and Stephen made another century and went on to beat me 10-5. Of course, Eamon was the first one up to shake his hand afterwards.

Hendry was relentless. When he won a tournament he

forgot all about it and got on with the next one because he was so driven to be the best. He was a terrible loser. He'd sulk like crazy if he lost, but that was proof of how much winning meant to him, how high he set his standards. I was like that to an extent but wish I was more like Stephen in terms of the way he dedicated himself so much to being better than anyone else. The facts speak for themselves: seven world titles, six Masters titles, five UK Championship titles, 36 ranking titles, more than 700 centuries and a total of nine years as world no.1.

There have been many great players who have lit up the snooker world with their skill and flair and nerve over the years but Stephen is the greatest of them all. Until his record of success is finally beaten that is how he will remain.

Ronnie O'Sullivan

I first met Ronnie when he was 12 and his dad brought him to Prestatyn to watch my matches. He was a great talent even then. We'd practise together in Ilford. His dad would send a taxi to pick me up from my digs and take me to his house where they had a table. Ronnie senior was a gregarious character, flash and cocky but also funny and warm. He was the sort of person you would be a bit wary of but also happy to be friends with and have looking out for you. Ronnie senior recognised how good his son was and wanted to give him the best possible chance to fulfil his potential, installing the table at home and getting him high-quality practice opposition.

One day I walked into their house and the entire dining table was covered in piles and piles of money, more than I had ever seen, which I guess was takings from his sex shops.

Ronnie senior looked like he'd just got out of bed. His hair was all stuck up and he was sat in his boxer shorts counting the notes. I was only young and pretty naive and said to him, 'You should shut the curtains. If someone walks past and sees all that money they might try and get in and steal it.' He smiled and said, 'Do you think someone's going to come in my fucking house and rob me? Don't you know who I am?'

Ronnie and I would normally play two 'best of 19' matches when we practised together. One time I beat him 10-2 and he said he'd had enough, that he was tired or had to do some homework or something like that. So I went out to get the taxi but realised I'd left my cue towel inside and went back to get it. When I reached the snooker room Ronnie was there practising away. He was a bit embarrassed but I just thought it was funny. He hadn't liked losing but he couldn't stop playing.

Ronnie was a terrific talent as a kid but he was very spoilt. His dad spoiled him rotten. He'd get frustrated because I wouldn't always play with him. If I'd promised someone else a game then I would honour that, even if Ronnie turned up. Everybody got on their knees when Ronnie and his dad came in because they were scared of them, but I didn't want to be like that. I didn't want to treat the other players with disrespect and I wanted Ronnie to understand why I was doing that, because it's one of the things he had to learn. It shouldn't matter how much money you have or who you are, you still have to have respect for other players, which at that time he didn't have because of his age and the fact he'd been so spoiled. I liked Ronnie and his dad and, yes, I was a bit scared of them too but I wasn't going to be different around them compared to how I was around the other people in the club.

We fell out eventually. He had friends that I thought were mine but they weren't, and we lost the relationship we'd had when he was just a kid and he looked up to me. He turned into a rival instead and he changed towards me when he became a teenager. He had an attitude whenever he played me for a long time, which all stemmed from Ilford. He'd got in with the wrong people, got into drugs and wasn't a very nice person for a while. I didn't speak to him for a couple of years over an incident with a girlfriend of mine but we eventually patched it up. We get on well enough now and sometimes talk about the old days.

Ronnie has grown up a lot since that time. Being deprived of his dad at the age of 16, when he was given a life sentence for murder, was very difficult and I can understand why he's had a lot of his well-documented problems since. I can't necessarily relate to it but I do empathise because he's had it tough despite his wealth and fame. I'm glad that Ronnie senior has finally been released because although he wasn't someone you'd ever cross, he was an entertaining guy and good to be around. It's nice that he can finally go round the circuit with Ronnie and share in his future tournament victories, bearing in mind how much effort he made to get him into that position in the first place. Now I've become a father I can appreciate the bond between a parent and their child, so it must have been awful for Ronnie not to have his dad there with him all those years.

I wouldn't like his life at all, not for one single day. He had to grow up very quickly and I think all the controversy has stemmed from suffering such a personal trauma in the public eye. Most people would be able to deal with something like that in private with their families, but Ronnie became a public figure at a young age and has had to play out his life in the spotlight. That isn't a comfortable experience when things are going well, never mind when you have such distressing events to deal with. He's had a life that has been difficult, with depression and all the other problems he's had, so it's a credit to him that he's won as many titles as he has and he seems to be in much better shape generally now than he was a few years ago.

I don't make excuses for the various controversies, like assaulting an official or walking out of a match, but the game benefits hugely from him being in it. The one thing I would say, though, is that he's got away with some of the things he's done and should have been treated more severely, like other players would have been in the same situation. The snooker authorities haven't hit him hard enough because he's such a big name and they don't want to lose him, but the rules should apply equally to all players, regardless of who they are or what they've done in the sport. Maybe he thinks the game wouldn't survive without him – even if he doesn't there are plenty who believe that – but snooker will always survive and he shouldn't be shown leniency just because of who he is.

Ronnie follows in the line of players that includes Alex Higgins and Jimmy White. I'd happily pay to watch him play. He's box office and the one player most people want to see.

His matches tend to be packed out and are often a rollercoaster ride of emotions for his fans, as well as for Ronnie himself. He's capable of absolute brilliance. He beat me 10-1 in the final of the 2001 UK Championship and completely embarrassed me, just destroyed me. As a player he doesn't have a bigger fan than me, but that doesn't mean he shouldn't be disciplined – like anyone else would be – if he puts a foot wrong.

What nobody can deny is that Ronnie brings huge excitement to the sport and has created many, many new fans from all over the world who might never have got into snooker were it not for him. He's an unpredictable character, a maverick, and you never know what he's going to do next so there is always a feeling of drama when he's playing. But he's also a genius, the most naturally talented player ever, and I love watching him play. No doubt about it, our sport would be much poorer without him.

Peter Ebdon

When I was living in Ilford Peter invited Stephen Murphy and myself to play for the King's Cross league team on Tuesday nights. It was an hour's journey on the tube but we were promised free practice and a free meal so, being potless at the time, we jumped at the chance. It seemed like easy money and we weren't bothered about the hour travelling there if we were getting free steak and chips. We coasted to the title but I've no idea what happened to the money. We never saw a penny of it but we still got our free meals and practice so we were content enough.

Peter was a big rival in those days on the pro-am circuit, which was thriving all over England. We'd play each other in quite a few finals but we never particularly got on. He's always been a deep person, very much a thinker, and he'd keep himself to himself, whereas I'd be having a laugh and a joke with the other Irish lads.

He was always a bit crazy, like he was constantly on the edge of doing something odd. I played him in the UK Championship one year in Preston and I was something like 8-3 up when he made a maximum break. He got down on his knees and burst into tears. He's someone who keeps all his emotions inside and then has to release them, which is why he became renowned for his fist-pumping celebrations. They wound a few other players up but I thought they were great and wish now that I'd done something similar. It would have proved how much winning big matches had meant to me because you do get emotional, but some players manage to keep it in and others let it all flow out. Peter is definitely in the latter category. All that shouting, 'Come on! Come on!' was good for the game, even if it rubbed some people up the wrong way. There's nothing wrong with showing emotion and letting the public know how much winning means to you.

Peter is the sort of player nobody wants to draw. He's as hard as nails and just never lets go, like a dog with a bone. He's even more dogged than I am. He takes his time and draws the matches out. You can't look forward to playing him because you know it will be a war of attrition. He beat me 9-7 in the Scottish Open final in Aberdeen in 2001 and the match went on for hours. He couldn't have dragged it out any

Above: In action during the 2010 World Open in Glasgow.

Below: Sharing a joke with Steve Davis and Mike Dunn at the Snooker Shoot-Out in Blackpool, 2011.

I spoke to Neil after he beat Graeme Dott in the final and advised him to enjoy his year as champion as much as he could. You never know if you'll ever be in that position again. I told him to take the trophy with him when he made personal appearances, show it off as much as possible. That's what I did and it always got a great reaction. Neil actually paraded the trophy at the Melbourne Cricket Ground before an Aussie Rules match in front of 80,000 people, which must have been a great buzz for him. I still get goosebumps thinking about the time I walked out with it on to the pitch at Old Trafford. There are few better feelings and it's like an extra reward for winning the title.

Neil has a fantastic cue action which remains strong in pressure situations. He's a great long potter and that makes him hard to play safe against, because you have to make doubly sure you've hidden the cue ball. He scores heavily when he gets in and displays a natural confidence around the table. Neil never gives up either, which again reminds me of myself. Against Martin Gould in the second round at the Crucible he was 11-5 down but fought back to win 13-12, a brilliant comeback that kept his bid to win the title on track and marked him out as a battler rather than someone who would roll over when he was up against it.

He's always had a slight swagger around the table, which seems to be an Australian trait. It's that confidence that is almost innate. It's not arrogance but it's a belief that they can walk the walk, and in Neil's case it's been proven that he can. It's a good thing to be like that as long as you have the talent to back it up. Neil is a little different – well, completely different

– in style to the ultra-cautious grinder Eddie Charlton, Australia's last great world-class player, but what they share is that will to win and doggedness that you need to be a champion, particularly at the Crucible where you really have to dig in for the long haul.

It's good for the game that he's reached the top. Hopefully it will mean we have a tournament in Australia, which would be another market that could be opened up just as China was off the back of Ding Junhui's success. Neil's progress may act as a catalyst to bring through other young players and persuade kids to get involved with snooker. The problem is that the climate in Australia is so good that most people play outdoor sports rather than wanting to be indoors for hours at a time playing snooker. Neil only took up the game because his father ran a snooker club. But now that he's won the game's biggest title and started to get some media attention in his home country, snooker might enjoy a resurgence down under. I could certainly think of worse places to play.

I like Neil and what he brings to the sport. He's a nice guy, open and friendly, and has a young image that will help snooker. He's not a big mouth or self-opinionated, just down to earth and natural, and his popularity will only grow the more success he enjoys.

Jimmy White

When I was 15 Kevin Norton, the tournament director at the Irish Masters, gave me a job as an usher at Goffs, which was a bearpit arena that played host every year to the very best players in the world. It was one of the most popular events on the circuit. The players were treated to the famous Irish hospitality and the public turned out in droves to watch them play. This was the 1980s and the top snooker players were like film stars, or so it felt to me at that age. I was there to show people to their seats but I was really just watching the snooker. I've always been indebted to Kevin because working there gave me an insight into the snooker circuit and allowed me to meet my heroes. He introduced me as a young, up-and-coming player from Ireland and asked the players to have a chat with me and pass on bits of advice. So I met and spoke to the likes of Ray Reardon, Cliff Thorburn, Dennis Taylor, Alex Higgins and Jimmy White.

That was the first time I met Jimmy and he's never changed. He's always had the common touch and it's genuine, which is why the public have taken him to their hearts. He's still so full of energy and can't sit still for two minutes because he's always got to be doing something, to be somewhere, having fun. He's full of life and that enthusiasm rubs off on whoever he's with.

I lost 10-9 to Jimmy in the 1992 Grand Prix at Reading, my first ranking tournament final. It was a great match and I have a picture of us from that night in my snooker room because it meant a great deal to me to play him at a big occasion like that.

I played him in the Irish Masters one time and went into a 3-1 lead. In the interval, he was running around looking for hairspray because his hair was so long at the front that he couldn't see properly. He must have found some because he came back and beat me 5-3. The atmosphere when I played him at Goffs was electric, completely unique. Just walking in you sensed it when you saw the car park full and the place packed with spectators. I had so much support. Of course, Jimmy had legions of fans as well and it made for an amazing, unforgettable experience.

I almost beat him in the quarter-finals at the Crucible in 1994. I'd come from behind to make it 10-10 and I was sat behind him and saw his hand shaking. I thought to myself, 'I've got him' but he stroked in a tremendous long red and went on to win 13-10. He had his disappointments but he never shirked from the big pots and that was one of the things I really liked about him.

As most people know, Jimmy lost in six World Championship finals. If he looks back now, he might want to change things he did in the past. If he had half as much determination as the likes of Davis or Hendry he would have been world champion for sure but everyone is made differently and Jimmy isn't made that way. He would never want to be like that. He couldn't just go to bed early the night before, or indeed during, a world final – he had to go out somewhere. It's in his make-up to always be involved in action because he'd go spare just sat in his hotel room.

A couple of times in those finals he had Hendry by the balls but he just didn't squeeze them. In 1992, Jimmy led 14-8 but Hendry came back, started to play superbly and ended up beating him 18-14. It was painful to watch if you were supporting Jimmy. Then in 1994 he missed a black off its spot in the deciding frame when it looked like he would finally beat Hendry and become world champion at last. Hendry, like the great pro he is, cleared up and that was probably Jimmy's last good chance to win it. Cheerful and resilient he might be but it's hard to pick yourself up after so many heartaches like the ones he suffered in the 1990s.

When I was in the final against Stephen in 1997 I had a 15-7 lead and I was thinking, 'You have him. Don't let him come back like he did against Jimmy – don't let him off the hook. You have to keep the pressure on and punish him.'

Jimmy hasn't been world champion but he's had a wonderful career and everyone respects him for what he's done in the game. There are no barriers with Jimmy. We can take the piss out of each other and have a laugh and a joke but then he'll go out and he's still a hard competitor. After he beat me at Prestatyn last season he put his arm round me and said, 'I know how hard it is coming here – it was for me as well – but you just have to keep battling.' He felt sorry for me because he'd been there and I appreciated that. He's become a good friend and he'll ring me up every now and again to see how I'm getting on, which isn't something most players would do.

Paul Hunter

Paul was a carbon copy of Jimmy White, except he was much better looking. They called him the 'Beckham of the Baize' and it was easy to see why. He seemed to have everything going for him – he was a great player, girls loved him, the papers took an interest in his life – but it was all just cut short.

Paul died of cancer in October 2006 when he was just 27, which was devastating for everyone involved in snooker because we all liked him and had assumed he would have many, many years ahead of him. He had seemed so youthful and perhaps the hardest irony of all was that you wouldn't meet many people who loved life as much as Paul. He always had a smile on his face and didn't take things too seriously. What happened to him was a tragedy.

We all went to the funeral and it was a very hard day, very touching and a fitting tribute but difficult. A lot of the players were in tears. I didn't know him as well as some of the other guys but I liked him a lot and admired him because he showed so much courage in the face of the cancer, never complaining and continuing to play despite the illness. It was sometimes hard to watch him turning up at tournaments and playing when he was obviously very sick but it must have been even harder for him to actually do it.

All the players liked and respected him. He was always a good laugh and wasn't someone who got too caught up with winning or losing at the expense of actually being a professional player. Paul just loved playing snooker and took everything else in his stride. At the Crucible one year I was due on the session after he had played, so I was in the dressing room he'd just used. I looked in the bin under the desk and there were two empty bottles of Smirnoff Ice that he'd had before he went out to play. I guess it relaxed him!

We played in the semi-finals of the World Championship in 2003 and I came back and beat him 17-16 from 15-9 down, which must be my best ever win. I can see him now, coming up to me afterwards and putting his arm around me to offer his congratulations. He was very gracious considering he had just missed out on a place in the world final having looked a certainty to make it. He must have been dejected but he said to me, 'You played great. Good luck in the final.' I knew he'd be gutted so I thanked him and said I was sorry for him but despite his disappointment, he seemed genuinely happy for me.

Days like the one spent at Paul's funeral are evidence that there are more important things in life than sport and results. His wife and little baby were there but Paul was in the coffin and that's what was really sad, what made me so upset. It was heart-rending but the game will never forget him.

CHAPTER EIGHTEEN

SUPPORTING MANCHESTER UNITED

Football has always been important to me. I always played in school and in the park and still love the game to this day. I play every Monday night in Ireland with my mates when I'm not in a snooker tournament and I absolutely love it.

In school, you were either Man United or Liverpool because they were top clubs but also had plenty of Irish players in their squads. My friends were all for United and I fell in line with them. My early hero was George Best. Years later I had a frame of snooker with him in the club because Eamon Dunphy had brought him in. George used to play a bit of pool in his local and was pretty good. He also played with Alex Higgins in Manchester, although Alex used to say, 'He was always nicking my birds.'

One time United were playing Tottenham at White Hart

Lane and I had a couple of pals over from Ireland, all of us looking for some tickets outside the ground. I met a guy called John Barry, who was a tout, and he recognised me from the TV. He said he could get me some tickets and, being a big United fan himself, came in to watch with us.

John was a great guy and we became friends. He used to live near Newport Pagnell services on the M1 so I'd drive there, pick him up and go to United games with him. This was in the early 1990s, just before United began to dominate and win all those titles. Sadly, John got cancer in his leg when he was a very young man and he died before he was even 40. I'm still good mates with his brother, Danny, and friend Micky Bennett. The four of us would always have a great time at the games, even if the result went against our team.

The United team of the 1990s were sensational and unstoppable. I used to love watching Mark Hughes, Roy Keane, Ryan Giggs and, in particular, Eric Cantona, who was an absolute legend. I was at the match at Selhurst Park when he kung-fu kicked the Crystal Palace supporter who was barracking him from the terraces.

I got a phone call once from Paul Ince's agent because Paul was a big snooker fan. Apparently he wanted to meet me because he'd heard I was a United supporter. I said, 'Well, I'll just check my diary.' It took me about two seconds to agree. I went into the players' bar at Old Trafford and had a chat with him and he was a top man, very much into his snooker. Through him I became friendly with some other players and I'd say hello to the likes of Roy Keane and Denis Irwin. One time David Beckham came up to me and asked how my snooker was going. Being a Londoner, he wanted to know about Ronnie O'Sullivan and what he was up to and even gave me his number to pass on to Ronnie so he could get in touch with him.

I still keep in touch with Incey. I get all sorts of texts from him along the lines of 'How did you miss that fucking ball?' and 'You're washed up, you're no good.' He gives me some terrible stick but I give it back to him.

It was interesting when I said to him once that it must be great going out on to that pitch in front of thousands of passionate fans and playing with some fantastically talented footballers. He said it was a privilege but he would prefer to do what I did because snooker is an individual sport and it's entirely up to you. In a team game, if some of your fellow players aren't pulling their weight you can get really frustrated and it can affect the result, but as an individual you don't have to rely on anyone else. I said we could always swap if he wanted.

When I won the World Championship I got to go out on to the pitch at Old Trafford and parade the trophy, which was a very special moment. It came about because the day after I won at the Crucible I did a press conference and mentioned that it would be great to take the trophy to Manchester United. John Parrott was a big Everton fan and he'd paraded it after he'd won the world title in 1991, although he had to take it to Anfield because Everton weren't playing at home on the last weekend of the season. All the Liverpool fans gave him a great reception, although the Tottenham supporters in the crowd were chanting, 'There's only one Jimmy White!' It had been Jimmy who John had beaten in the final. JP told me how great it felt to take the trophy to Anfield, where he'd watched matches as a kid, and I wanted a piece of that.

So it went in the newspapers that I wanted to take it to Old Trafford and my management very quickly got a call from United inviting me to come along. A week later myself and Bill King went up to Manchester and met Martin Edwards, the chairman. He gave us a tour and I met Alex Ferguson, who is a huge snooker fan and has a full-sized table in his home. I was introduced to Sir Bobby Charlton in the directors' box and had photographs taken with the Premiership trophy. Then I went to meet the players but it was a bit awkward because they were sat down having their lunch ahead of the match and I didn't really want to intrude. The first one to stand up and welcome me was Eric Cantona, who was the captain at the time. He was a great giant of a man and he came over and shook my hand and congratulated me on winning. I was amazed he'd even heard of snooker, let alone known who I was.

I then had a chat with some of the other players. It was an incredible experience. I was in awe of all of them but when you talk to them you realise they are just ordinary lads like you who happen to be in the spotlight. A lot of footballers like to relax by watching other sports, including snooker, and also by playing snooker or pool. I had a sense of pride that they recognised me but my mouth was hanging open because I'd be thinking, 'Look, there's Ryan Giggs and there's Paul Scholes.'

We had a chat and then Martin Edwards asked what I should do with the trophy. Alex Ferguson said, 'He's going out there' and pointed to the pitch. 'Send him out there with it at half-time and let him show it off.' So I did and it was a beautiful moment, one I'll never forget. It was another occasion where I felt I should pinch myself because I was a United obsessive ever since childhood and then here I was, on that famous pitch, listening to the Old Trafford roar and it was all for me.

Sir Alex is such a snooker fan that when he announced his retirement in 2001, I asked John Parris to make him a cue. I brought it up to a game to hand it over, even though the previous week he'd announced that he'd changed his mind. The chief executive, Peter Kenyon, sent me up to Alex's room and I gave it to him. I said, 'Alex, when you do eventually retire, you can play with this.' He was chuffed to bits. Dennis Taylor told me once that he was at Alex's house one time playing snooker and that he showed him the cue and said Ken Doherty had given it to him, which was nice to know.

Most people see Fergie getting het up at big matches but he's a really friendly guy and a huge sports fan. A few weeks after I met him I was playing at a tournament and he phoned Dennis to say that every time I was breaking off two reds came out and I was leaving them on. He told Dennis to tell me to break off from the other side. He was trying to manage me!

The best match I've been to was when United won the Champions League against Bayern Munich in Barcelona in 1999 with two late goals. I was so excited to be going that, amid all of that, I'd forgotten my passport. It didn't matter going from Dublin to Gatwick but I couldn't fly to Barcelona, so my pals Danny Barry and Mick Bennett had to go on ahead and I had to get my passport flown over to me on the next flight. I finally made it to Spain and got to the match. The end was amazing.

United were a goal down with only minutes to go but goals from Ole Gunnar Solskjaer and Teddy Sheringham brought us victory. A lot of fans had left early, assuming the worst. When I got back to the airport there were loads of people who had missed all the drama. Even George Best left the stadium before the end.

Another brilliant match was in 2009 when United won the Manchester derby against City 4-3. The atmosphere was the best ever and we won it with a Michael Owen goal in the last minute. The drama of it couldn't be written. It had to be seen to be believed. To be in the crowd for a match like that, to be part of a group of fans experiencing such exhilaration, is just an amazing feeling.

Football has changed since I was a kid. Back then there were hardly any matches on television; now there are often several games on TV in one day and you get to see all the really big matches live. The money has gone through the roof but I don't mind players getting paid huge wages. I'd rather they got the money than the directors. It's good to see players being rewarded for their skill but I don't like ticket prices going up to pay for it. Ordinary fans shouldn't be penalised because they are the heart of any club.

I'll go anywhere to watch United. It feels like an escape. It's something outside of snooker that I can enjoy and be passionate about. I definitely made the right choice when I picked them as a school kid.

CHAPTER NINETEEN

BACK TO THE CRUCIBLE

Sheffield, 9 March 2010

What a difference a year makes. Twelve months ago it was here at the English Institute of Sport that I missed out on the televised stage of the World Championship for the first time in 15 years. After all those seasons when I just had to turn up at the Crucible, seeded through to the final stages as a member of the top 16, it was a culture shock to have to play in the qualifiers. I had little confidence going into the match with Gerard Greene because my form had been so poor all season and although I tried to raise my game, it just wasn't there. I lost 10-5 and the season was over: it meant I wouldn't be part of the 17-day drama that is the World Championship.

It was a bleak moment and a slap in the face, a kind of wake-up call. I knew it was a question of either sliding away

167

into obscurity or pulling myself together and stopping the decline. So I'm delighted to have qualified for the Crucible a year on from that dark period in my career.

It's cruel in a way playing the qualifiers here in Sheffield, just a few miles from the Crucible Theatre itself. You feel that it's almost within touching distance but driving past it on the way home when you've not qualified is heartbreaking. Then again, I'm not sure leaving Prestatyn having just lost is any more fun.

I'd fallen so far down the rankings that I was required to play two matches to qualify. The first was against Jimmy White, one of the last players I wanted to come up against because he's such a good friend and I'd be willing him on against anyone else – not least in the World Championship, a tournament in which Jimmy has reached six finals but never won the title. He's still a huge draw and would be as popular as ever if he did make it through.

The snooker table is no place for sympathy, though. I had to block out all my personal feelings and treat it as any other match. Jimmy would have to do the same because I'm sure he would have been wishing me well against most other players. As he said himself, 'It's just business.'

He had been unlucky with the scheduling because his previous match didn't finish until after the midnight before our game began at 10am. This obviously didn't give Jimmy much chance to come down from the elation of winning, but the other side of that coin is that at least he'd had a match in arena conditions and some valuable ranking points in the bag. I was coming in cold, although everyone is under pressure here. This is the World Championship very few people see: there are no TV cameras here. It's dog eat dog to get through to the Crucible and although there's plenty of good snooker played, it's mainly just scrapping for every frame. It means so much to everyone.

I managed to get ahead early on against Jimmy. I'd been nervous before the match but settled down relatively quickly. It wasn't one of my best performances but that doesn't matter. All that matters at the qualifiers is getting the result. I went on to beat him 10-3. As he always is in victory or defeat, Jimmy was gracious and wished me well. It was a huge personal disappointment but it says a lot about him that he can still take the time to offer some words of encouragement to the guy that's just beaten him.

My win over Jimmy put me into the final qualifying round and a match against another of my best friends on the circuit, Joe Swail. He was another player I wouldn't have picked for the same reasons as drawing the Whirlwind, but once again I had to set friendship aside and just get on with the job. It's all part of being professional. There's an old snooker saying: 'Play the balls, not the man.' It's not always easy to do that but it should be your aim, to just stick to your game and not take any notice of the person you are playing.

What you don't want at the qualifiers is a close game, particularly in the World Championship. Frankly, all those nerves, all that tension isn't good for the heart. If you win a 10-9 match you're on top of the world but to lose one is an almighty kick in the guts. So I was delighted to beat Joe 10-1 to clinch my place in the Crucible draw. It was a scoreline nobody, myself included, would have predicted before the match but I relaxed quickly and Joe struggled. It just wasn't his day.

What gives me confidence is that I didn't just scrape through. I beat two good, experienced players and beat them convincingly. I'm not kidding myself this is world-beating form and I still have to improve, but to be one of the 32 players in the hat for the draw is a wonderful feeling, the complete opposite of the miserable way my World Championship ended last year.

Whatever happens now, at least I now know that I'll end the season at the Crucible. Whoever I play and however far I get, at least I'm part of it.

CHAPTER TWENTY

THE HIGGINS SCANDAL

One of my best friends on the circuit over the years has been John Higgins. What I've always liked about him is that he seems to get on with everybody. There's nothing hidden with him. If he doesn't like something you or someone else has done he'll just come out and say it rather than go behind your back. Of course, it all changes when he gets on the table. He's one of snooker's fiercest competitors with a better record than most but he's managed to mix his genuine nice guy persona with that hard edge that you need out in the arena, which isn't easy.

That's why I was absolutely devastated when I found out the *News of the World* were running a story on the eve of the 2010 World Championship final, alleging that John had agreed to fix matches for money. It was a front-page world exclusive with plenty more details inside, plus a video on the newspaper's website. John and his manager, Pat Mooney, had been secretly filmed in the Ukraine by journalists posing as businessmen, apparently agreeing to accept a six-figure sum to manipulate results in tournaments that comprise the World Series, which was a concept they set up to take snooker around Europe, where it has grown in popularity in recent years.

I played John in the World Championship final in 1998 and although it was close going into the final session, with him leading 13-11, he stepped up a gear to beat me 18-12. He also made what was then a record 14 centuries in the event and has proved on many subsequent occasions why he's regarded as one of the best players to ever pick up a cue.

In our years on the circuit I've found I can talk to John about anything, whether it's family, because we both became fathers, or football, as he's a Celtic fan and I follow them after Man United, or poker. John is interested in most sports and you can always chat to him about them. He's the sort of person you don't mind finding yourself next to on a long haul flight, because he's always got something to say and you can have a laugh with him without there being an edge to it or any thoughts that something that happens privately will spill over into the match arena. Even if you disagree with him on something you won't fall out over it.

That was the John Higgins I liked and thought I knew, so to be confronted with these damaging headlines was a complete shock, a total blow. I was in the hospitality room at the Crucible for Betfred, the World Championship sponsors, and their media relations man Mark Pearson was emailed the front page of the *News of the World*, which read 'Snooker Champ In Bribes Scandal'. As more information started to come in I began to feel sick.

I was in Sheffield working for the BBC alongside many other people who help to make the tournament happen, from the media to the sponsors, officials, table fitters, Crucible staff and of course the spectators. It's a community of dedicated people and by the end of the championship they are all exhausted by the long days and seemingly endless snooker. On the Sunday morning when the full details of the story emerged, everyone was in shock. They were in a haze of disbelief. It was the eeriest feeling I've ever known at a snooker tournament, as if there had been a death in the sport. There was a silence around the building instead of the buzz of anticipation that usually greets a World Championship final.

The story couldn't have come at a worse time. There was a real feeling that snooker had turned a corner with Barry Hearn taking over as chairman of the governing body and all the enthusiasm he brought to the game, so to be confronted with damaging allegations about a much-admired player was about the worst thing that could have happened. Everyone had given two weeks of their time, working long hours to make the championship a success, and it felt like the ultimate kick in the teeth. It completely overshadowed the world final itself, which was unfair on Neil Robertson and Graeme Dott, as all anyone could talk about was what would happen to John.

We knew it had gone round the world. Television news crews had parked their vans outside and newspapers from every corner of the globe were reporting the story. I felt sorry for Steve Davis who had brought the championship alive when he beat John 13-11 in the second round. It was an incredible result and brought the tournament a huge amount of attention but I knew that people would now be pointing the finger – wrongly – at whether or not that match was contested honestly. Steve was very low that Sunday and he had my full sympathy. Even though he knew his victory was honest, what happened to John subsequently must have taken some of the shine off it.

If you had to predict a player to become involved in something like that then John would not be high on the list of likely candidates. He wouldn't have been on the list at all. It seemed completely out of character and in any case a huge risk for a player who was at the time world no.1. I've always been close to him and didn't know what to think. I tried to call John and sent him a text to see how he was feeling because I couldn't begin to imagine what he was going through. It was such a public humiliation and I never heard back from him, I guess because he was so embarrassed and didn't want to talk to anyone. He must have wanted the ground to swallow him up.

Barry Hearn immediately suspended him, which meant he missed out on several events at the start of the following season. Eventually, an independent tribunal accepted John's claim that he had just been pretending to agree with the match-fixing plan because he was scared for his safety. That had been his first line of defence and it never changed, even though many simply didn't believe it. As the evidence emerged it became clear that Mooney had led him into a situation where his entire professional career was put at risk. John was naive and he was stupid. He fell for a trap and has paid a very heavy price for it.

He was cleared of the main allegations but still found guilty of failing to report an approach to match-fix and of giving the impression that he would engage in corruption. He was fined £75,000 and the suspension was extended to six months, but it meant he could return to playing reasonably quickly but with his well-earned reputation in pieces.

I was pleased to see him back because although I think he was very stupid, I don't believe he is essentially dishonest. No money changed hands and I don't believe it would have done. But a lot of people in the game, including players, felt John basically got away with it. Many of them can't understand how he could have got off as lightly as he did. Some players have told me they don't think he should be back playing at all. People have come up to me in the street and said the same thing.

There had been a precedent. Quinten Hann was secretly recorded by undercover reporters agreeing to throw a match against me in the China Open. He was subsequently banned for five years so John may consider himself lucky, although Hann didn't mount any defence.

There was evidence in John's case that wasn't made public and, in the end, it was an independent hearing that decided his fate – not that that will silence those who believe he should have received a longer ban. I think it would have been awful for snooker had John been thrown out of the game, because the whole sport would have looked corrupt in the eyes of many and they would have stopped watching. I accept John was stupid not to spot the situation he had been put in but I don't think he's a cheat. I still count him as a friend.

I can't imagine what John's life would have been like if he had been banned for longer. He's a family man with a wife and three children and he would be completely lost without his snooker career. He must have spent so many miserable, anxious days and nights waiting for the verdict.

If you look at John's career and what he's achieved then he has to be considered as one of the greatest players of all time. He's certainly one of the toughest I've ever played against, along with the likes of Hendry, Davis and O'Sullivan. I hope he's still remembered that way but the scandal has inevitably meant that his reputation has suffered and there will always be people who will point the finger at him.

The scandal surrounding John was part of a wider problem that the authorities had failed to tackle over a number of years. It seems to have intensified with the growth of internet betting and as tournaments have decreased, so have players' earnings and one or two of them have been tempted to cheat. It happens in every sport and snooker players are not immune to the temptations that come their way.

It's a virus that has to be eradicated from the game. The sport is nothing if people don't believe that what they're watching is honest. The only good thing to come out of the John Higgins saga is that players will be so scared now about getting involved in fixing that they'll think twice. Barry Hearn has set up an anti-corruption unit and is promising tough punishments for any players found guilty in the future. It's headed by David Douglas, a former Metropolitan Police superintendent, and Lord Stevens, an ex-Met commissioner, so we're in good hands. They should root out any cheats and deal with them appropriately. We need the sport to be clean.

I've played matches where I've suspected my opponent isn't trying or is even deliberately attempting to lose frames. I've also been approached to lose on purpose, not by other players but by figures outside the game trying to make a killing through internet betting. I've never been tempted to do it. Not once. It would be a betrayal of everything I've dedicated my life to. Your career and reputation are much more important than any financial gain you can get from throwing a match. It worries me that some of the younger players who don't know much better have been tempted. They are putting their entire careers at risk if they let themselves become involved in anything like that. I would never condone cheating and I'm glad Barry Hearn has introduced a zero tolerance attitude towards it.

I don't believe for a minute that cheating is widespread in snooker. There have been a few incidents over the years that have raised suspicion but snooker is a lot more honest than many sports. You only have to look at the etiquette in the arena where players routinely own up to fouls unseen by the referee. But there have been people lurking in the background who have got hold of players and told them they can get away with making extra money on the side, and there's always a worry a few of them may have fallen for it.

The John Higgins case was a wake-up call for the sport of snooker. It jolted everyone into taking action, finally, to stamp out match-fixing and the temptation to cheat once and for all. John himself has had to work hard to rebuild his reputation within the game and with the wider public. He knows that snooker's integrity too was damaged by what happened in the Ukraine but hopefully from now on players will realise they have a responsibility to behave properly as the professional sportsmen they are supposed to be.

CHAPTER TWENTY-ONE

THE FAME GAME

One of the positive side effects of being a sportsman is that you get to meet people from other walks of life who you admire. I've been lucky in that I've met a number of high-profile people, particularly from Ireland.

Dublin is a cool place in the sense that you don't have tabloid newspaper photographers running around taking pictures of anyone remotely famous as happens in London, even when that 'fame' comes from having appeared on *Big Brother* or something equally shaky. Ireland is a less intrusive place. I remember watching Billy Connolly walking down Grafton Street and people noticing him and nudging each other, but nobody went over and interrupted him. The lads from U2 are the same. They used to drink in Dockers, a pub down by the docks, and nobody would bother them. They were treated as ordinary guys.

And they are down to earth when you meet them, but they are still heroes of mine. I grew up listening to their music and they are still pretty much the biggest band in the world. That's a great feather in the cap for Ireland.

I've met them a few times after being invited backstage to concerts. I managed to pluck up the courage to go and shake hands and tell them what a big fan I was. The funniest meeting was a couple of years after I won the World Championship when a group of us were with my friend Paul Sheehan, who runs Sheehan's, a pub in Chatham Street. We'd had a few beers and he had to close his place, cash up and then we were going to head down to Lillie's at the bottom of Grafton Street. Paul pulled the shutters down at about 11.30pm and went through the cash register while we put on some U2. One of my pals went across the road to a pizza place to get us something to eat and came back to tell us that The Edge was in there. So we said, 'You should have invited him over for a drink.' It's not every day you get a chance to have a lock-in with one of the world's most famous guitarists. We stood peering through the windows waiting for The Edge to leave the pizza place and, when he did, we opened the door and shouted, 'Edge, Edge, come and have a few pints with us!'

He politely declined. He probably thought it was some bunch of drunks and didn't want anything to do with us. For all he knew, anything could have happened to him. So we closed the door again and thought nothing more of it. Then a few minutes later there was a knock at the door. And there was The Edge stood there with Guggi, a member of the Dublin school group who gave Bono his name, and Simon Caverty, a writer, and we invited them in.

The U2 music was still on and we felt a bit stupid playing it in front of him, so we took it off and got some Frank Sinatra on instead. We had a drink and a chat, and it turned out The Edge was really into snooker. He was asking me about Alex Higgins and Jimmy White and he couldn't have been nicer.

An hour later we were all pissed. The Frank Sinatra CD was coming to the end and the last track was 'New York, New York' and we were all up in a huddle, dancing and kicking our legs. It must have looked a ridiculous sight but it was one of the great evenings.

Not long after that The Edge bought an hour's free snooker tuition with me at a charity ball. He paid seven grand for it. To be honest, I'd have paid seven grand just to give him the lesson, although he's so busy with the band that it still hasn't happened. If he's reading this now, I'd still be happy to show him the ropes!

A week or two after the lock-in I was walking past the Shelbourne Hotel just as Bono was coming out. He was with his wife, Ali Hewson, who used to be in college with a good friend of my mother's, so I'd met her a few times and said hello to her. I'd met Bono in passing and he knew who I was. He said, 'Hey, man, I hear you had a good night with The Edge. Sorry I missed it.'

It was weird, really, that I was just chatting like that with Bono. People say it's not good to meet your heroes but he's always been perfectly friendly to me. When I played Mark

Williams in the 2003 world final I came back from 11-5 down to 12-12 after the third session and when I turned on my mobile phone afterwards there was a message from him. He'd got the number from someone and he said, 'We're all watching you here, you're doing great, go on and win it.'

I've been to a number of their gigs. The first one was at Croke Park, I think it was 1987, and I've also seen them at Earls Court, Wembley and at the Point in Dublin on New Year's Eve, which was one of the best gigs I've ever been at. They have some amazing songs but they're also great showmen and put on an unbelievable performance.

What always surprises me is that footballers and pop stars, who seem to have the best jobs in the world, are so often interested in snooker. Paul Ince is a good example. It didn't compute with me that a footballer might be in awe of a snooker player. Anyway, we got on great and it turned out he knew some of the guys from Ilford Snooker Centre. He was fascinated by the sport and wanted to talk about snooker all the time while I wanted to ask him questions about football. One of the reasons he liked snooker so much is because it's a sport where you are completely alone, out there in the middle with nobody to help you. If it goes wrong it's your fault and nobody else's. Similarly, if you win, the glory is all yours.

I could see his point but I know as well as anyone that snooker is a lonely sport. With team mates you have company and banter and they become almost like family, whereas we're on the road all the time. You can get close to other players but they are still rivals. It isn't the same as being part of a band of brothers.

Sir Alex Ferguson told me that when he first signed Incey he played him on his table at home. They'd play for a tenner a frame but they were so competitive it was like pints of blood. Alex said there was one time when Paul had brought his wife and she watched them play after dinner. When he missed one particular ball he blamed her for putting him off. That shows how sportsmen hate losing even in a social setting. When I play football with the lads it's like the FA Cup final. You just want to win all the time. It's a desire that's instilled in you, a competitive spirit, so that no matter what you're playing, you want to succeed. You want to play properly and hate it when people don't give it 100 per cent. I think most if not all leading sportsmen and women are the same.

Speaking of leading sportsmen, I've known Padraig Harrington, twice Open golf champion, for a long time. We came to the fore as juniors in our respective sports and met each other through winning awards as 16-year-olds. We've followed each other's career and I have to say Padraig has been a great ambassador for his country. He's probably the best sportsman ever to come out of Ireland.

I've only ever played him once at golf. You can probably guess how that went. We've never played snooker but we have had a few games of tennis. We had one match that was best of three sets, with a tenner to the winner. Padraig beat me two sets to one and took the tenner off me. He folded it up into a little square and said he would keep it in his wallet as a reminder for the next time we'd play. His wife told me he kept it there for about a year and then one day he was in a petrol station and found he had no cash in his wallet other than that folded-up tenner. It broke his heart having to spend it because he wanted to play for it next time.

I played with Padraig in a pro-am at the Belfry and have seen him play at the Irish Open and the Ryder Cup, but I don't like to get too close and intrude on his personal space because golfers, just like snooker players, have to be in that mindset where they are concentrating on the event and their game and nothing else. The last thing you need is people making demands on your time and interrupting your focus. To win the Open once is a great achievement but to make a successful defence shows how good a player he is. He has terrific character under pressure and bags of self-belief. He's worked a lot on the mental side of the game, something that is so important in individual sports where it's basically all up to you and how you handle yourself. That's helped him to win titles and move from the group of also-rans who have never won a major to someone who has won three in the space of a couple of years.

I was invited to the BBC *Sports Personality of the Year* show in 1999, which was a celebration of the previous century of sport. Muhammad Ali was there. He was someone who I had always admired and I was desperate to meet him. I was in the hotel beforehand with Ian Doyle but I'd forgotten to bring my camera and didn't want to miss out on a picture with Ali if the chance came along, so I said I'd go and buy a cheap disposable one. Ian was adamant that it wasn't necessary as there would be plenty of photographers at the event and I could easily get a photo from one of them. Not for the first time, listening to Ian was not the best decision I ever made.

It was a tremendous evening full of big names but for me it was all about Ali. His life and career dwarfed that of anyone else there that evening, and that's saying something because the room was full of sporting legends. It's not normally something I would do but when I saw him free I rushed up to him. It went through my mind that I might never get the chance again. So I went up and shook his hand. I told him it was my greatest pleasure to meet him and thanks for all his memories. He didn't have a clue who I was but it didn't matter: I touched the hand that shook the world. He was suffering from Parkinson's disease, which caused him to shake, but he was still sharp. When he presented an award to Lennox Lewis he said that looking at the modern boxers he was thinking of making a comeback. It had everyone laughing. But, of course, I'd listened to Ian and never did get a picture with him.

One of my other big heroes was George Best and I did get to know him. Indeed, I played a frame with him when I was about 18. George always followed snooker on the TV and, as you would expect, was great company. I have a picture of him in my snooker room and one of Alex Higgins underneath. Alex was practising in the room one day and he was looking at his own picture. I said, 'Look, Alex, there's one of your old pals, Georgie Best.' He looked at the photograph and said, 'Poor Georgie, what a waste.' If only he'd followed Alex's lifestyle!

I suppose I've become a well-known face in Ireland because snooker has been on the TV so much over the past couple of decades. I get recognised and it's nice when people take the time to come and speak to me. I remember Noel Gallagher from Oasis once saying that one of the best feelings in the world was having someone come up to him asking for an autograph. It's true because it means they respect you and the vast majority of people are friendly and only have good things to say. It particularly touches me when people shake my hand and say they remember where they were when I won the world title in 1997, because it shows that it meant a lot to them as well as to me. I appreciate the interest people have taken in my career and the support they've given me. It's not a strain or an imposition to take a few minutes just to chat to them, pose for a photograph or sign something, nor should it be for any player. Without the fans snooker wouldn't be a top television sport but I've seen some players be really ignorant to them. That's not how I was brought up. When I was young my mother told me not to pass anyone on the way up because you're bound to meet them on the way down.

Top snooker players are celebrities, especially the more established names who have been around since the 1980s. Dennis Taylor and Willie Thorne have been on *Strictly Come Dancing* and Jimmy White toughed it out in the Australian outback on *I'm a Celebrity... Get Me Out of Here!* There are a lot of those shows and I can't stand most of them, but I watched Jimmy in the jungle and it was hilarious viewing. At one point he had to wear a red Lycra suit – I've still no idea how he got in it – and there was one challenge where he kept getting dumped in water full of gunk for getting the answers wrong in a memory test. He really enjoyed it and fair play to him. Not everyone would want to humiliate themselves like that but he came out of it really well, finished in third place, lost three stone and ended up getting the wildcard to the Wembley Masters due to the boost in his popularity. He also liked the solitude: there were no mobiles or computers or anyone making demands of him.

I think that would be a good experience but I'm not keen on the other shows. *Strictly Come Dancing* looks like a lot of fun and Dennis and Willie loved it, but dancing isn't my thing. I wouldn't want to stand on my partner's toes. *Celebrity Big Brother* doesn't appeal either. Ronnie O'Sullivan is a big fan of it but it looks boring to me. You're basically just in a house doing nothing.

One thing I would like to get involved with is Soccer Aid, which is an annual England v Rest of the World football match organised by Robbie Williams. I love football and it would be an opportunity to play with and against some of my heroes. They play the match at Old Trafford. What could be better than that?

One thing sports people have to be careful of when they go on these shows is not making themselves look so ridiculous that they end up taking the shine off their achievements and being remembered for taking part in a reality TV show rather than what they've won. People would lose respect for you and you'd lose respect for yourself. It's part of the balance of being a sportsman. You want to use whatever profile you have for good, to help charities and also to carve out opportunities that will help you sustain a living when your career is over.

But the world of celebrity is a fickle one. I've no idea how someone like David Beckham can stand the circus he lives in, with photographers following his every move, his haircuts and clothing being analysed and his private life intruded on. There's no respite from it. At least he has a genuine talent. So many wannabe 'celebrities' chase fame without actually having achieved anything other than appearing on a TV show, sometimes only briefly. Then they become part of that whole scene which just perpetuates itself.

It's not a life I envy and it's one of the reasons I'm so fortunate to live in Ireland. Here, most people just see me as Ken. I'm not put on a pedestal and I'm not being constantly bothered. When people do come up and chat to me it's usually just brief, friendly and may involve a picture or autograph, which I'm happy to supply, and then I'm on my way again. That suits me just fine.

CHAPTER TWENTY-TWO

LIFE OUTSIDE SNOOKER

It's important to do other things and fill your leisure time with something other than snooker. There's enough pressure, stress and worrying that accompanies a high-profile individual sport without having to think about it every minute of the day. So I have a wide range of hobbies and interests to help me take my mind off the green baize.

I play 11-a-side football with a bunch of friends every Monday night. We have a great laugh and it can get pretty competitive. We have a good range of ages from those in their twenties to one player who is 60. It's terrific fun and a way to wind down away from snooker.

I used to play two games a night. I'd play with my mate Nicky English, a well-known hurler from Tipperary, and he had a team who would play from 8 to 9pm. Then I'd jump straight in the car and play for another team from 9.30 to 10.30pm. In the end, I had to knock the first match on the head because it was time for Christian's bath and then bedtime.

Graeme Dott broke his wrist playing football in Shanghai and it has worried me that I might take a knock that could hamper my snooker. Graeme missed two tournaments when he suffered his injury and it played havoc with his ranking position. I'm very lucky in that the worst I've done is a groin strain or pulling a hamstring. Sportsmen tend to be competitive in whatever they do. We can't help ourselves, it's just the way we are. Thankfully, though, the lads on Monday night don't go in too hard, otherwise I could be in real trouble.

I've played a few charity football matches as well with the likes of Liam Brady, Paul McGrath and Ray Houghton. I've played against Ronnie Whelan, Ian Rush and Trevor Steven but I've yet to play in a match at Old Trafford, which would be an ambition realised. I did play in a game at Celtic Park and John Higgins was on the other team marking me. I managed to lose him and score, which was incredible.

I also play quite a bit of golf. I'm captain of a skins society and every year we have a Masters event that lasts four days with a green jacket for the winner. We've been going to Spain for the past few years. My handicap is 14. I don't get to play as much as I'd like to, which obviously makes it difficult to improve. I've always liked golf and am in awe of players like Tiger Woods, who make what is an extremely tough, skilful game look effortless, but my time tends to be taken up with football or poker, which I've got heavily into these past few years.

I get invited to quite a few poker competitions and do OK

but the top poker lads, as with the leading personalities in any sport, are seriously good. They just seem to know exactly the right time to make their move. I got through to the last 56 in the Irish Poker Open from a starting field of 700 and I'd love to go to Las Vegas for the World Series, which both Steve Davis and Stephen Hendry have played in.

Again, it's the competitive instinct. I love the thrill of testing myself and going all out to win. If you saw me on the soccer pitch on a Monday night I'd be the one shouting and screaming, giving out to people. If I take something up I want to play it to a decent level. Well, to be honest, I want to win. Although it's supposed to be fun, it's always more fun when you win, or at least when you've given your best. I know some people will find that hard to relate to and say, 'It's only a game.' It might only be a game to them but to me it's a chance to excel at something, to rise to a challenge and come away with a sense of satisfaction that my efforts have been rewarded.

If I'm not playing sport I have various cultural interests. Art is a big passion of mine, Caravaggio in particular. It started when I was doing up my house. There was an art gallery right next to our school when I was growing up. I used to get the bus past it every day but never went over and had a walk around. It was only when I got into my twenties that I started to appreciate art. I wanted a print on my wall, just something a bit classy that would look nice. From there, I began to understand that paintings told stories and were documents of history as well as just being pleasing on the eye.

Caravaggio became a passion of mine when I went to the

National Gallery in Dublin. One of their most prized possessions is his painting *The Taking of Christ*. It's such a beautiful painting, so striking. It lit up the whole room. I got into his story, which is tragic. He was an aggressive character who got into a fight in Rome and apparently stabbed and killed someone, although it was never known whether or not he was actually responsible. Rather than await trial, he panicked and fled on a boat from Sicily to Malta, where he remained in exile. We've had a lot of tournaments over the years in Malta, where he painted many of his pictures for rich families. The Pope was going to pardon him because he wanted him painting in Italy. Caravaggio got back to Italy but he died on the beach before he could receive his pardon. He was only in his mid-thirties, so he had many more beautiful works to create. He sounded like an electric, uncompromising character – a bit like Alex Higgins! And, like Alex, he was a genius.

Every painting has a story. There's no point going into a gallery and just staring at the paintings. You can appreciate them more if you understand the history of the piece and what the artist was trying to say. I've learned about light and moods and how artists use different shades to develop themes. I realise many people will be surprised that a snooker player is fascinated by art but I don't think the creative world and the sporting world are that far removed. We are both striving to achieve something and I suppose in some ways we are both trying to make our marks on history.

My wife Sarah shares my appreciation of art. Some of our favourite times are walking around Merrion Square in Dublin where all the Irish artists hang their paintings on the rails and sell them every Sunday. It's a beautiful stroll on a nice sunny day and you get to appreciate the great talent on show. These people may not be famous but they are creatively gifted in a way I admire. It's wonderful to see their skill and dedication come to fruition. I've seen the Sistine Chapel and also the *Mona Lisa* in the Louvre and the talent required to bring these paintings to life is unbelievable.

I'm not artistic at all. I could just about paint the railings of a gate but that's about it. My brother, Anthony, was very good at art at school. He wasn't that great at the other subjects and became a butcher but he's really talented. I wish he'd followed that up.

I'm not big into TV, although I enjoy comedies like the *Catherine Tate Show* or *The Office*. I much prefer the cinema. I love Woody Allen. I could never grow tired of his films. They have a style of comedy that's different to those of any other filmmaker and they still make me laugh. I love thrillers as well and I can sit through any of the James Bonds, but to be honest I'll watch just about anything. Friday used to be cinema night when I started going out with Sarah. We'd try and go every week, although that's no longer the case now we're parents but we still get there when we can.

I'm not keen on sitting on a beach but I've always been interested in history, so if I go to a place I want to learn the historical facts about it. I think you appreciate somewhere more if you know how it has developed.

Whenever I go away I'll take a book with me. I used to read a lot of fiction. It was down to Jeffrey Archer, who was appointed president of the World Professional Billiards and Snooker Association a few months after I won the World Championship. I had to go to Westminster and pose for pictures with him on a snooker table that had been specially erected. He was a novelist as well as a politician and it was one of his, *Kane and Abel*, that got me into reading regularly. I don't blame Archer for this but fiction didn't really appeal to me, because my interest in history meant I gravitated towards books that were factual and that you could learn from. Biographies became my thing and I always have one on the go.

When it comes to music, U2 are a big passion of mine. They are one of the greatest Irish exports and have become probably the biggest band in the world. I've been to many of their gigs and it's always a phenomenal experience. Frank Sinatra is another great favourite of mine and I've started listening properly to the Rolling Stones and the Beatles, who were around when I was born.

If it's karaoke night I'll get up and sing – reluctantly I should stress – 'Father and Son' by Cat Stevens or 'If Tomorrow Never Comes' by Garth Brooks. I'm not sure how many people would want to hear me doing them, though.

CHAPTER TWENTY-THREE

FAMILY LIFE

I was out one night in 1999 with friends in Dublin and we went to a place called Cafe Insane, which was a big super-pub, a huge place with a beautiful bar. We were five or six guys out on a bit of a pub crawl, nothing out of the ordinary. It would have been my dad's birthday and so a poignant day for me. Little did I know that evening would change my life. It was the night I met my future wife, Sarah.

The place was pretty busy and we were just having a bit of craic, telling stories and relaxing. Sarah was sat close to us with one of her friends, a guy, and we assumed they were boyfriend and girlfriend so didn't even say hello. It was two or three deep at the bar and I was struggling to get served. I looked round and there was Sarah, who is only five feet two, so however hard it was for me to catch the barman's eye, I knew it would be a lot tougher for her. I turned to her and said, 'You're going to need a stepladder to get a drink in here.' Then I turned away and thought, 'Jeez, what have I said?' It seemed like an insult and I was gutted because I'd just met this beautiful girl and already messed it up, so I just walked back to the lads with the drinks.

Even though I was just trying to break the ice, I felt dreadful. I went over and apologised to her but she said it hadn't bothered her and we started talking. I said something like, 'Aren't you going to introduce us to your boyfriend?' – basically testing the water to see who this other guy was. She said he wasn't her boyfriend and that he was her brother, although that turned out not to be true. We all ended up in a big circle and were chatting away. I was a little shy with her but there was one guy in particular, John McHugo, who would have been in his fifties but acts like he's still in his twenties. He's great fun and a real laugh and took a fancy to Sarah. He found out she was studying psychiatry and asked her out to dinner. I only found out later that another pal of mine, Randy Burns, a professional golfer, had said to John, 'Back away, Ken likes her.'

Sarah didn't know who I was or anything about snooker, which was refreshing because she didn't have any preconceptions of me. She had come over from Australia so there's no reason why she would have had any knowledge of me or my career. I invited her down to Lillie's nightclub and at the end of the night we chatted and got on really well. Sarah doesn't drink so she gave me a lift home and I asked her for her phone number. We started going out after that.

The funny thing about meeting in Cafe Insane is that, like Sarah, her parents don't drink alcohol so her mother thinks we met in a cafe, not a bar. Her family are Indian so for our first date I took her to a new Indian restaurant that had just opened up. I'd never eaten a curry before but I was hoping it would impress her. It was a relatively short courtship. I'd previously been with a girl for four years and in a couple of relationships after that, but I felt so comfortable with Sarah, so happy. For whatever reason we clicked.

We got married in Melbourne, Australia on 29 December 2001. It was in a place called Emu Bottom Homestead, which doesn't sound too great I know, but it's a beautiful country farm in one of the suburbs. There was a farmhouse-cum-function room and it was surrounded by beautiful hills and valleys and various wildlife. Eleven members of the family came over. I'd invited everyone but it's such a long way. We got married outside. It had rained all the way up to the big day itself, then the sun came out for us and after that it rained again the next day. We were so lucky and I felt like it must be an omen.

I had a tailed morning suit made by Louis Copeland and Sarah looked beautiful in her white wedding dress. But I was really, really nervous. It was almost like walking out into the Crucible. I knew I loved Sarah but it was such a big step. Needless to say, I'm glad I went through with it!

Sarah's family didn't know much about me, although they knew they could look me up on the internet. They don't have the pay-per-view TV they would need to watch snooker in Australia. Sarah's father is a doctor but also a pastor in the local church and does a lot of missionary work, including building schools and churches. This is obviously a more important way to spend time than watching me play snooker. I did give them a DVD of me winning the World Championship but I don't know if they've seen it or quite what they'd make of it because it's an alien sport to them. They are happy for me if I'm doing well but as long as I'm good to their daughter, that's all that matters.

It's hard for Sarah because she chose to stay in Ireland while her family are over in Australia. She was always going to go home until she met me. It's harder now we have our son, Christian, because they don't get to see him and that's a strain on her as well. We used to go over in the summer and at Christmas but it's too much for Christian to fly all that way so they come over here now.

It's difficult to sustain relationships when you're away on the circuit so much but Sarah has her own life and career. Her job as a psychiatrist takes up a lot of her time so it's not like she's left rattling round the house when I'm away. She works extremely hard and is as focused on her career as I am on mine.

I often joke that the best thing about being married to Sarah is that I get free consultations but it's definitely a help to be with someone who is so good at listening. She doesn't know much about snooker but she has a great understanding of the psychological impact that certain results have on me. Players tend to sulk for a few days after a bad defeat. It's hard to avoid because you've spent so much mental energy getting yourself up for the match that you're bound to suffer an adverse reaction if it all goes wrong, particularly as defeats are so public. Some snooker wives probably think, 'Why don't you cheer up? It's only a game' but Sarah understands the pressures I'm under. She's someone I can talk to about how the mind works and she is also a good motivator. She understands why I need to go to practise in Sheffield and that I need to watch what I eat and exercise to stay healthy and give my game everything.

Sarah is strong, intelligent and speaks her mind, which I respect in anyone. She doesn't come to tournaments because she has her own life and career that takes up her time. Denise Higgins, John's wife, once joked that I wasn't really married because she never met my wife at tournaments but Sarah has her job to think about and also doesn't want to come over and upset my routine and focus. After all, I wouldn't tag along to her work.

In December 2008, I became a father for the first time when Christian was born. I always thought that winning the World Championship was the ultimate high possible but nothing compares to fatherhood.

The day he was born, Sarah felt her waters breaking and so I got her and her parents into the car and we headed off to the hospital. I dropped her outside and went off to park. She looked funny waddling across the road, like Charlie Chaplin, even though it was obviously such a serious day. Inside the hospital, she got panicky and was telling me to leave her alone. It was scary, not least because when her mother gave birth to Sarah's brother, Charles, she almost died through complications. Sarah was saying things like, 'Get away from me! This is all your fault!'

She was operated on and the baby duly arrived. We'd been to the last scan and I didn't really want to know the sex, although Sarah did so that she could do up the room. As we were looking at the screen the nurse said, 'Oh, look at that.' It kind of gave away that it was going to be a boy. I didn't mind either way, as long as the baby was healthy. Some of the scans scared me because they ascertain whether there will be complications but thankfully we cleared all of those.

We'd thought of names in advance. Sarah's mother kept on putting forward Joshua, a good Biblical name, but I knew a few Josh-es already. Sarah liked Tristan but Peter Ebdon has a son with that name and it would have looked a bit odd if we'd gone with it as well. So we came up with Christian, which Sarah's parents were happy about. You can't get much more Biblical than that.

When he was handed to me I found tears coming to my eyes. I held him for 20 minutes and my arms were starting to shake. It was the most beautiful feeling I've ever experienced, more so than winning any snooker tournament. His little face was looking back at me and I knew that he and Sarah would always be the most special things in my life.

I miss Christian terribly when I'm at tournaments but when I'm at home I probably get to spend more time with him than people who work regular nine-to-five jobs. He loves animals so we take him to the zoo and he enjoys going to the park as well. He also loves Hamleys toy shop and he's a lot of fun. I'm a bit of a kid myself so we get on great.

The first few weeks after he was born were quite difficult and tiring but we were lucky that we had Sarah's parents staying with us. We kept messing up changing his nappy because although you can be shown something all day long, until you actually do it you don't really know how to, but we soon got the hang of it. We were a little nervy because we wanted to make sure everything was right, so it was like walking on eggshells, but Christian soon settled into life at home and we soon settled into life with him.

People say becoming a father adversely affects your game but I'm not sure if that's really true. Some would argue that sportsmen, who have to be pretty ruthless, selfish even, lose a slight edge when they have children. This may be true but I don't believe that becoming a father affected my form. I'd argue that because you're playing for someone else it gives you even more motivation. Maybe you're not quite as focused but I'd like to use Christian as an inspiration. I'd love Sarah to walk out at the Crucible with him in her arms, just like Alex Higgins's wife did when he won the title in 1982.

I've taken Christian to my snooker table a few times and he loves rolling the balls around on the carpet. I've had him on the table chasing the balls and giggling away. I don't think I'd like him to follow in my footsteps and become a professional, though. For all the glamour and rewards it can be a tough, lonely life. You experience a lot of ups and downs and have to make sacrifices and be quite single-minded to succeed. Only the top five per cent really make a good living from the game and the rest struggle.

Obviously if he did take up snooker I'd give him as much help and support as he needed, but it would be hard for him being compared with his dad. I'd like him to do his own thing but as long as he's happy and healthy and stays away from drugs and trouble, he can do what he likes. I know I'll always be proud of him.

CHAPTER TWENTY-FOUR

POTTING ALL OVER THE WORLD

One of the best things about being a snooker professional is the chance it has given me to travel the world. The circuit is still largely based in the UK but more recently a boom has occurred in China and there's also one happening in Europe, so I will hopefully be getting full use of the passport in the years to come.

I've always been interested in other cultures and I try to see a bit of whichever place we're in, rather than just sit in the hotel like some players do. It's important to try and occupy your mind instead of allowing yourself to get bored and homesick. It astonishes me when I hear players moaning because they have to get on a plane to play in a tournament. We're supposed to be a world sport and not just a British game. Also, a lot of people would love to be in our shoes, travelling to all these interesting places to play the game we love.

One of my first overseas tournaments was in Dubai, which was a much-loved destination for the players because it mixed great weather with considerable hospitality. You would always hear about what a great time they'd all had in the lap of luxury. I hadn't qualified the year before but when the other lads came back they all had these lovely Cartier and Rolex watches as presents from the sponsors, so when I got through to the final stages I couldn't wait. I thought this was the big time, having expensive gifts thrown in my direction. I was rubbing my hands together in anticipation.

I was only wearing a cheap watch because I knew I'd come home with a better one. I played Graeme Dott in the first round. I always take my watch off before I play and having beaten Graeme I went off to do the press conference before realising I'd left the watch at the table. So I went back into the arena but there was no sign of it. I wondered if the referee had picked it up but he hadn't. I asked around but nobody had seen it. Worse still, it emerged that the sponsors wouldn't be giving out watches that year, so having gone there expecting an expensive one I came home having had my own watch stolen. It wasn't quite the trip to Dubai I'd been hoping for.

At the same time there were tournaments staged regularly in Belgium and Holland, two countries that loved their snooker. You would always receive a warm welcome from the people there but, sadly, the powers that be couldn't keep the run of events going. More recently the major events have been screened regularly on Eurosport, which means interest right across Europe is huge again. It's made a massive difference to the sport because these are the markets that can help us expand snooker's appeal. Television is so important to driving interest, as we saw in the UK and Ireland in the 1970s and 1980s. TV can create new fans and, as Eurosport is available in more than 50 countries, that's potentially many millions of people.

The most enthusiastic country for snooker in Europe seems to be Germany. They held ranking events for a number of years in the 1990s but now interest has exploded beyond all expectations. I can go out to a restaurant in Germany and be recognised, as can players from various sections of the ranking list, whether they're a top name or not. The German snooker public have a genuine respect for the players and the game itself.

Some of them seem almost obsessed. I was playing Barry Pinches in the final of the Paul Hunter Classic in Fürth when a spectator suffered a heart attack. He'd fallen down on the floor and his wife beside him started screaming. An ambulance was called and he was taken away to hospital while the match was delayed for around 45 minutes. We came back to resume the game and as I broke off in the second frame I looked up to see his wife coming back into the arena. I assumed she'd forgotten something but she sat back down in her chair so she could watch the rest of the final. I'm not sure anyone could believe it but it shows the German dedication to snooker!

China is another country where the fans love their snooker. When Ding Junhui beat Stephen Hendry to win the 2005

China Open at the age of just 18 they had a viewing audience of something like 110 million. It's unbelievable to think there would be that many people watching a snooker match. Ding's victory has sparked a huge boom and there's a considerable increase in the number of snooker clubs cropping up. Many millions of people are playing regularly and also watching on the TV. It's the world's biggest country in terms of population and businesses are pumping money into sponsorship of tournaments. I think the number of these events will grow and grow because there's no doubt the demand is there.

In China, you quite literally get the red carpet treatment. Their events are launched in fine style with players arriving as if for a film premiere. It's surreal to those of us used to just pitching up in a car to play in British events, often barely noticed. Over in China you can be chased down the street by screaming fans. It's a lot to adjust to but I love it. They show their passion for snooker, which is what we need.

The only problem I see in China is that the tournaments aren't readily accessible to many ordinary people who would like to come along but can't afford to. Ticket prices seem high and it leads to a strange situation where the arenas aren't packed with spectators, even though they could sell them out many times over if they lowered their prices. People prefer to watch on TV because wages aren't high and it's a massive financial outlay to come along. If this could be addressed then I think it could only benefit the game as a whole, because the more fans enjoy the live experience, the more they are likely to continue following snooker.

Before the explosion of interest in China, the leading Asian country for snooker was Thailand, due to James Wattana's rise to the top. James was one of the game's top players for the best part of a decade from the late 1980s. The fans there really took to snooker and welcomed us to their country many times until the interest waned as James's own game started to decline.

I won the 2001 Thailand Masters, a ranking event, but one of my best times playing anywhere outside the UK and Ireland was when I represented Ireland in the 1996 World Cup in Bangkok. It was a three-man team also featuring my pals Fergal O'Brien and Stephen Murphy, with Michael Judge there as a reserve. It was a great two weeks, one of the best experiences I've ever had as a snooker player.

In the semi-finals we were up against England. Each match was a single frame and it ended up going into a decider. I had to go out and play Ronnie O'Sullivan, who at the time wasn't a very nice person to know. He was cocky and full of himself and tried to take the piss out of me at the table. He played a good safety shot and tapped the table, as if to applaud himself. I found that disrespectful. I beat him in that last frame shoot-out. At the end of the match I had a black off its spot but I decided instead to roll up behind it and was really tempted to tap the table myself. There were amazing scenes afterwards. The Irish lads piled in and hugged me. It was wonderful because, as a player, you're usually an individual. You're representing yourself more than your country so to be able to play for Ireland was special. We lost in the final to the Scottish 'dream team' of Stephen Hendry, John Higgins and Alan McManus but there was no disgrace in that. We'd exceeded most people's expectations by reaching the final.

I think the reason we did so well was because we had such good camaraderie between us. We all got on well, even those who'd come to support us. My mate Finbar Ruane had come over to cheer us on. When he told his girlfriend he was planning to go to Thailand for two weeks to watch, she said he could forget about going without her. So he told her he'd go to Spain instead to play golf. The semi-finals and final of the World Cup were shown on the BBC and they had a camera in the players' room, where Finbar could clearly be seen watching. Willie Thorne, commentating, said, 'There's a good friend of Ken Doherty, Finbar Ruane, who has come over to Thailand to watch the snooker. His girlfriend thinks he's in Spain playing golf.' When he came home after two weeks in Bangkok he found all his car tyres had been slashed.

If Ireland and Scotland had a good team spirit, England was the opposite. They were more like a collection of individuals. The English side comprised Ronnie, Peter Ebdon and Nigel Bond. There was one match when Nigel was going out to play having lost a few frames already and I heard Ronnie shout after him, 'Come on, Nigel, get your act together for fuck's sake!' O'Sullivan and Ebdon respected each other but didn't really get on. I think the difference in the way the teams bonded was the reason we beat them, which was a huge upset considering the talent they had on their side, with three players ranked inside the top five in the world.

Barry Hearn wants to expand the game outside Britain even more and I'm all for that. What's needed in all of these countries is more international players. Ding's success has brought along other Chinese players such as Liang Wenbo, and they help drive the popularity of snooker in China because the public have local heroes to cheer on. James Wattana led the way in Thailand and Neil Robertson can hopefully do the same in Australia. Maybe one day Germany will have its own world-class player. It would be good to think the top 16 in five or ten years' time could be dominated by non-British players, which might also help stimulate interest in the UK because it would tap into the 'us against the world' mentality that goes with so many sports.

I'm certainly looking forward to many more foreign forays in future years. It helps to remind you that snooker really is a global game. There are amateurs in all corners of the planet and they all have the same dream that I did as a boy: to turn professional and be world champion.

CHAPTER TWENTY-FIVE

THE WORLD TURNS

Sheffield, 4 May 2010

It's the morning after the night before, and a very late night at that. After a lengthy final, Neil Robertson beat Graeme Dott 18-13 to become world champion for the first time. Neil is the first non-British winner since I won the title in 1997 and only the third from outside the UK since the event was first staged in 1927. His mother flew over from Australia to be with him and there were some great scenes in the arena afterwards as they celebrated.

The final was poor. Both players seemed very tired, Dott especially. I've never been particularly close to Graeme but I was very impressed with the way he handled himself throughout the tournament. He probably played the best snooker of anyone to reach the final. In fact, he played even

211

better than he did when he actually won the title in 2006. It was a valiant effort but even a player with his strength of character can't do anything about exhaustion. He had a long, drawn-out semi-final against Mark Selby which he won 17-14. That meant he played 15 frames on the Saturday before the final, whereas Neil saw off Ali Carter 17-12 and played only five frames on the same day.

Maybe that had an impact on the final result, although Neil was still the worthy winner. One thing that impresses me about him is how well he stands up to the pressure, and it's never greater than on the last night at the Crucible. He emulated one of my comebacks from 2003 when he beat Martin Gould 13-12 in the second round, having trailed 11-5 going into the final session. Some players would have just gone through the motions in that situation but Neil gave it everything and got his reward. Fair play to him and I hope he enjoyed his time as world champion as much as I did. There's no better feeling in the game.

To be honest, though, the standard in the final was so low that it gave me a bit of heart. I was watching it thinking, I could beat these. I'm sure many other players felt the same way, although it might have been a different story had we actually got there and been as knackered as Graeme and Neil. Even so, although there are a great many players capable of producing good performances in the circuit these days, I don't feel that the standard has risen dramatically at the top level since I was world champion. There are just more players now able to produce that standard.

My Crucible run ended in the first round. After qualifying,

I genuinely didn't care who I drew because it was just a great buzz to be in the hat at all having missed out in 2009. That said, there were three players I would have liked to avoid: Ronnie O'Sullivan, John Higgins and Mark Selby. And guess what? I drew Selby.

Ronnie has the capacity to blow you away and John is the game's best all-round player but Mark isn't far behind him in that department. He's a class act and a big occasion player, as he proved in January when he came from 9-6 down to beat Ronnie 10-9 in the final of the Wembley Masters. There aren't really many flaws in his game; he can knock in the big breaks but also has a good tactical brain and can mix attack and defence to great effect.

So I knew it would be a tough match but I was also determined to enjoy being back at the Crucible. One of Barry Hearn's innovations since becoming chairman has been to play music when the players enter the arena. You get to pick the track you want and it's supposed to represent your personality. Being Irish and a big fan of their work, I was going to go for a U2 song but I decided instead on 'The Irish Rover' by The Pogues and The Dubliners. It's the sort of song that gets the crowd going immediately and brought a smile to everyone's face.

When I entered the arena, I knelt down and kissed the floor of the Crucible stage. I'd thought about doing it but wasn't sure if I'd go through with it or not until I actually got out there. The song and the atmosphere seemed to be right for me to do it. I'd wanted to demonstrate my pride at being back in Sheffield and that felt like the perfect way of doing it. It got the crowd on my side but ultimately it made no difference to the result. Mark beat me 10-4.

It was close early on but I missed a good chance to make it 3-3 and the match went away from me after that. Once eliminated, it was back to the BBC commentary box and studio. These are long days for everyone but it helps when you're part of such a friendly team and the punditry keeps me involved with the tournament. The highlight for me was commentating with Willie Thorne on the final session of the second-round match between Steve Davis and John Higgins. Steve won 13-11 – an astonishing result and a heart-warming one too. Everyone in the game knows how much he loves snooker so to see him pull off such an incredible victory gave us all a boost. It also gave players like me hope that there are still plenty of victories ahead of us.

Both Willie and I got tense watching in the commentary box. It was a pleasure to have a front row seat like that for what was the match of the tournament. We had to remain impartial but I was genuinely made up for Steve when he won. It was his 30th Crucible appearance, which is a record that will take some beating, and outside his six titles it was one of his most memorable.

On the first day of the semi-finals Steve and Dennis Taylor played an exhibition frame to commemorate the 25th anniversary of their famous 1985 world final, which went down to the final black. It was a very funny occasion and proved what entertainers they are. It was the sort of thing that gives snooker a good name and shows the worth of using former players and established names to bring something different to major tournaments outside the serious competition. The public certainly enjoyed it.

The season is now over and I look back on it with pride from a personal point of view. It wasn't world-beating stuff from me but I managed to stop the worrying slide down the rankings. Having started way down in 44th place, I've got myself back into the top 32 and so will have to play one qualifying match rather than two in next season's ranking events.

My ambition at the start of the campaign had been to halt the decline and turn things round so I was going in the right direction again. I qualified for the final stages of three of the six ranking events and therefore played on TV in each one. OK, this isn't mind-blowing form but it's a vast improvement on where I was a year ago, when my whole career was in doubt. In the other three tournaments I didn't lose a first-round match and that helped me climb back up the rankings.

So I've ended the season with something to build on. I don't want to stop here. I believe I can get back in the top 16 and that's what I'll be working towards now. It's been a tough season because I've had to make sacrifices. I knew I had to play in as much as I could to try and get my sharpness back, and that has meant more time away from home than I would have liked, but you get nothing out if you don't put the effort in.

The bottom line is that I'm ending the season with a positive frame of mind compared to last year when it was all negative. What this year has taught me is that I still have the drive and the desire to play snooker at the top level. I'm not going to take it easy now because there's still a lot of work to do. I know that time is limited now that I'm in my forties, but I do believe I can still cut it at the top level and I'll be aiming to prove that in the years to come.

I look back at that time sitting on Prestatyn station, tears welling in my eyes, and feel satisfied that I've managed to pull myself back from the brink of retirement. I've proved to everybody in the game this season, but most of all to myself, that I'm not finished and I'm not a pushover. I can't wait to play again.

CHAPTER TWENTY-SIX

HOW OTHERS SEE ME

This book is my story of my life and career but I also wanted to include contributions from those closest to me, namely my family and friends. They know me best and can help to build a picture of me, where I've come from, what I've achieved and my failings. So I asked my mother, my brothers and sister, my wife and some snooker pals to give their insights into the Ken Doherty they know – good and bad.

ROSE (mother)
I came to Dublin when I was 17 and trained with the nuns in Muckross. After getting married I became a mother and Ken was the third of our four children. He was a happy boy but there were some unhappy times during his childhood because the owners of our house wanted us out and wouldn't rest until they got their wish.

The John F. Kennedy Library was to be built nearby and the owner of the property where we lived wanted to sell it because he thought it would make a nice profit, but first they had to get rid of us. They did everything they could to get us out. It's very upsetting to remember it. We had to go to court one time to get keys to get back in because they'd changed the locks. For ten days we had to climb through the window. We'd come back at night and they'd throw the bins into the hallway. They'd call us dreadful names and let the water run onto the floor. They made our lives a misery. Ken was only a young boy of three or so at the time but they'd kick his toys around. This went on for over two years until we got a new place.

As a child, Ken was well behaved but he did like to torment his brothers and sister by playing jokes on them. He liked making mischief and still does but I didn't have an ounce of trouble with him, apart from having to pull him out of the snooker club. He worked hard at school and got good grades, even though he sometimes fell asleep because he'd been out the previous night playing snooker. The masters would ask him a question and even though he'd been asleep he could still answer.

I was quite strict with my children but I've been lucky with the way they've turned out. Anthony was the wild one – I'd be out looking for him at one in the morning – but Ken stayed out of trouble. Football was a big passion of his. The manager of the team he played for in Rathmines came down to my house to beg me not to let Ken give it up when he decided that snooker would be his sport. They really rated him highly. I said I couldn't stop him and that he'd have to give up one of the two sports as he didn't have time to play football, snooker and concentrate on his school work. I was more keen on him knuckling down for school than the sports in any case. We lived close to Jason's and at the time I thought snooker was just something for the boys to do. I had no idea it would come to be Ken's career. He loved all sport, not just snooker and football but tennis and swimming as well. As a boy he was always active, always adventurous. He couldn't simply sit still. He had to be doing something.

I didn't want him to be a snooker player. He was so good at school and I worked at Trinity College, where the children of staff members could get in if they got certain grades. But Ken had his heart set on snooker and nobody was going to talk him out of it. He'd started winning small trophies as a junior and his dad once said to him, 'Maybe some day you'll win a big one,' but sadly he never saw him do that. I wasn't interested much in snooker but I was glad he enjoyed it, although to me snooker clubs were for youngsters who didn't want to go to school.

I sometimes had to literally drag Ken out of Jason's. I'd give him a time he'd have to be home by but he would get so involved in the games that he'd stay on and I'd have to go down there. He had the mumps when he was young so he was confined to bed. I went up to take him a hot drink but he wasn't there: he'd gone out to play snooker. I think he won as well.

Ken used to say he practised seven or eight hours a day but if that was true he'd have been a lot better. It was more like three or four hours and then he'd be on the machines in the club. He always seemed to win on those as well but I didn't like Ken playing on them at his age. There had been a young lad of 17 or 18 who committed suicide by crashing his car into a wall after spending all his wages on the machines. I hate card games too and I'm not happy that Ken spends time playing poker today.

We had little arguments over the years about the time he was spending playing snooker but the only real problem we had was when he wanted to go away to England. Originally he'd left school and I said, 'You're not going to spend all your time in snooker halls.' Ken went back to school to spend another year studying history and passed his exams, but by then his mind was set on going to the UK. He didn't have a father to advise him so it was down to me to try but I couldn't talk him out of it. Once he was set on pursuing his snooker career I accepted it because I wanted to support him, but I was very upset that he was leaving home.

I always trusted Ken. I knew he wouldn't be involved in any trouble but I was concerned about his welfare. Thankfully Eugene Hughes was very good to him. He looked after him and became like family so that eased my mind, but I did worry about him in London. It was difficult not being able to keep an eye on him but he always phoned me regularly and seemed to be happy.

I never watched him play, not even when he turned professional. I just get too nervous. I'd watch his matches on video afterwards but only if he'd won. He was on for a 147 at Wembley and his sister Rosemarie called up the stairs to tell me to come down and watch it, but I replied, 'I'll come back down if he gets it.' And of course he didn't.

If Ken was playing in a big match like a final I'd usually go out walking or cycling. I might go to church to say a few prayers for him. I'd have to stay away until the match was over, even though I'd be thinking about it all the time. I'd try to put it out of my mind but it would always be there, tormenting me. When he was in the World Championship final in 1997 I was in church and a man came in and put two fingers up as in a victory sign. That's how I found out he'd won. I watched it back on video but I was still nervous for him, even though I knew he was going to win. I had the trophy on top of my television set for a year. I was so proud of Ken that he'd achieved what he'd always set out to. He'd put his mind to it and got to the top.

He still enjoys his snooker. He's never lost that love for the game. I know he doesn't win so much these days but he's got married and settled down and become a father, and maybe he doesn't have the same drive as he once did. I think he'll remain involved in the game, maybe by opening a snooker hall or teaching youngsters, because it's in his blood.

He's as good as gold to me. He still teases me and messes around but it's all good natured and he's always there if I need him. I'm very proud of Ken.

SEAMUS (brother)

To understand Ken, you have to understand his mother. After moving to Dublin to work she gathered enough money to buy a three-storey house, which she wanted to open as a guest house, but she was gazumped and so was unable to proceed. That broke her a bit and is still a source of regret to her. She'd been working with my father and he asked her to marry him. They were in love and she said yes, even though she maybe had different dreams for herself. My father lost his job with the Marist Fathers when she was seven or eight months pregnant with me so she got on a bus to Coolock outside Dublin, which was considered the country, even though she couldn't afford the whole fare there. She got to the priest's house by getting on and off buses, pretending she was on the wrong one and so on, and begged the priest to keep her husband in employment or she'd reveal certain things that had been going on in the house. That's the determination, the strength she has, never to give up, and Ken has shown that same fighting spirit in his snooker career.

Growing up with the O'Connors persecuting us was horrible. They would repeatedly turn on the water to flood the place, they took a tin of paint and threw it all over the bathroom and even squeezed all the toothpaste out of the tube. Our father was working for a hotel and was on nights so he would come home at seven in the morning to try and get some sleep, but the two of them would pound on the door to keep him awake and he would have to go to his family home instead.

All the trouble meant that we formed a close family group. Our mother used to work cleaning in offices at night but when she became pregnant with Rosemarie she obviously had to take time off to have the baby, so I would go and do the job for her. We just had to survive somehow. Both our parents were working every hour they could, so I would look after Ken while they were out. We remain every bit as close today.

He'll come to me to talk over things that he probably wouldn't raise with anyone else. The trust has been there since day one.

Ken and Anthony fought a great deal as kids, although they got over that eventually. It was nothing you wouldn't see in any other family. We were just normal really, no different to any other Irish family, but our lives were torn apart when our father died. That teatime we were sat at the table having our tea. Rosemarie was going to a concert in Muckross and our mother explained she was unable to take her, so Dad said he would instead. On the way back on Ranelagh Road he got a great pain in his leg. It had happened before because of the clot he had and he got embarrassed about having to stop for a few minutes while the pain calmed down. He reached into his pocket, gave Rosemarie money to go into a shop, and collapsed. Myself and Anthony were watching the disaster movie *Earthquake* on the TV and someone knocked on the door to tell us what had happened. It was horrifying. He died a couple of days later in hospital.

It was almost like our mother knew that something like that would happen, because when we got the new house not that long before she had said, 'What do I have to give up for this?' It was almost too good to be true after the previous two homes we'd had and therefore the feeling was that something would go wrong. She was widowed at 49 years of age.

I was 21 and had to assume the fatherly role within the family. When Ken started travelling round Ireland as an amateur I would go with him and also accompanied him to England for international matches, just to keep an eye on him, not that he was ever any trouble. He was always focused on playing.

223

I used to go in a snooker club called Nat's, but you had to be a certain age to enter and Ken was too young. Just at that time Jason's opened and we started going in there. Ken had natural ability but he also worked on his game and took advice from some of the older players and coaches rather than thinking he knew it all, which was a key reason he progressed in the way he did. He was prepared to learn from the more experienced players and take on board their advice and wisdom. He respected their viewpoint and his game developed as a result.

Ken seemed to have an inbuilt talent for sport and anything competitive. Jason's would run competitions on the pinball machines and space invaders. They'd have a first, second and third prize and invariably the family would collect all the money. He was great at soccer and asked me once, when he was a teenager, whether he should choose football or snooker. My answer was that it was up to him but that you could have a longer career at snooker, which didn't depend on physical fitness.

One of the reasons so many people get on with Ken is that he can talk to anybody. Our mother used to take in down-and-outs and they'd sleep under the stairs. When we lived in the house with three rooms she took in a woman from the home for the blind for six weeks to give her a holiday. Our parents gave up their own bed for her and slept on the couch. We had an open door for people who needed help and that extended to the wider area. Our granny lived with us for a while and would go out and feed the milkman, the postman, the guy round the corner who ran the petrol pump, anyone who wanted feeding. That's the sort of community it was and it meant Ken grew up with the worldview that everyone was important and they should all be shown equal respect and consideration, something he still believes to this day.

Mother wasn't an academic person but used the money she made from her various jobs to pay for private tuition. I went to school on a Friday night and Saturday morning to boost the level of education I was receiving during the week. She instilled in Ken the need to knuckle down and get his grades, so she wasn't exactly over the moon when he told her he wanted to go to England to pursue his snooker career. I was on Ken's side. As far as I was concerned he had no choice and had to go. I knew he was serious about snooker and I knew from what everyone on the Irish scene was telling me that he could make it big in the sport. I told him he should go. He eventually did and there was no turning back after that. I went over a few times but basically let him get on with it. He had to go his own way, as you do in life. It's one of the reasons we stay away from tournaments because I went to a few and it put him off, having to consider us rather than concentrating on what he should be doing.

He's done well for himself for someone who has come from such humble beginnings. He's the type of person who would have been successful at anything. He has an ability to make money, which is a survival thing he's picked up from our mother. Even as a kid he was earning thirty quid a week – twenty from Jason's and ten from a paper round – which I wasn't even getting from an office job.

He doesn't get stressed. He's easygoing, which our father

was as well. He takes his time over everything, has no sense of urgency. He's a terrible person to go shopping with because he takes forever. I'm more impulsive, I want to get in and out as quickly as possible, but Ken has to inspect everything on offer. He's never been one to hurry.

Losing isn't something he's got used to dealing with. He goes into himself for a couple of days afterwards and it's almost like there's been a death in the family. We'd let him stew for a bit and then try and gee him up, tell him there'll be more tournaments and support him that way. We'd try and reassure him that worse things happen in the world.

The 1997 world final was a horrifying experience. Watching on you can't do anything to affect the result and you're so tense because it means everything. I'd seen my young brother take his first steps into snooker when he couldn't even reach the balls and there he was in the world final. It was unbelievable but so nerve-racking that I couldn't wait for it to be over. In some ways the fact Ken was ahead most of the way made it worse, because victory was within his grasp. I remember Ian Doyle, his manager, saying on the TV at one point that it was in the bag for him, which to my mind was done to fire up Stephen Hendry, the golden boy of the management stable. Sure enough Hendry started to claw his way back from 15-9 down to 15-12 but Ken hung on. We were all so proud. He'd achieved everything he could at amateur level and now had done the same in the professional game. It was sweet for us all, knowing what he'd gone through to reach the top.

He probably should have won it again. Maybe his commitment slipped after winning the world title. 2003 was his big chance and I felt he was robbed because nobody has ever made more of an effort than he did that year. Anthony and I went over and at the official reception while Mark Williams was sat eating his starter, Ken was being mobbed by players and officials, congratulating him on his great run. That spoke volumes to me.

I think his family has kept Ken grounded. I remember him coming back the first time after spending six months or so in Ilford and he seemed to be talking with a slight English accent. I pulled him aside and reminded him he was Irish. It hasn't happened again. The Irish people will always support their own but they won't let you get ideas above your station. We don't fall out in the family. We might have arguments but once they are done a line is drawn under it and we move on.

These days Ken lives a pretty simple life and is happy, which is all you can ask for. He's a family man and enjoys that. He's adapted seamlessly to being a father and I suspect he would like more children, which is another reaction to his own childhood when the house was always full of people. Our extended family, our aunts and uncles, were always affectionate with us and promoted fun. I suppose they didn't have much money so they tried to make things as happy as they could for the kids. One thing we never lacked was love. Ken has done well from snooker but hasn't gone mad with money and he hasn't forgotten where he's come from.

ANTHONY (brother)
The truth is, Ken and I never used to get on. I'm five years older than him, the middle brother, and it's probably true that

I resented him a bit when he came along, in that childish way. I remember him when he was a kid of two or three. He had these eyes that would just stare into you. He never seemed to blink and it frightened me. So with that and a bit of envy, I suppose I grew up not really liking him. When he got older, we'd fight. I'd always pick on Ken because he'd annoy me. He wound me up, whether he meant to or not, although a lot of the time he did mean to. He just had this way of getting under my skin and we'd fight constantly until he was a teenager.

I'd been the youngest brother until Ken came along and in my eyes he took the attention away from me. In my teenage years I went off the rails a bit. I became involved with a bad crowd and started getting into trouble doing daft things when I should have known better. Looking back, I was probably seeking the attention from elsewhere that I felt I'd lost at home. I'm not proud of how I behaved because it created problems for my family. The rest of them didn't cause any at all so I was like the black sheep. Some nights my mother would be walking the streets into the early hours looking for me to take me home but our elder brother, Seamus, was well behaved and thankfully Ken took after him and not me.

Ken applied himself at school and always behaved properly at home. He was well mannered and also talented at most sports. He had a lot of energy and a kind of will to be the best at whatever he did, even when he was just a kid. It was strange because he was a happy-go-lucky kid but as soon as he was involved in a sporting contest this competitive spirit kicked in. Whatever sport it was, he applied himself. He was into tennis and once played a guy who was known in Dublin to be a bit of a player. Ken beat him 6-0, 6-0, 6-0. He also played football to a good level for Rathmines Boys and won player of the month and then player of the year something like five times, so that shows you how well regarded he was. He could possibly have made it as a footballer because he didn't just have talent but also drive and desire. It wasn't that obvious, not like he walked round thinking he was the best at everything, but it was in there, inside him. But he was like that with anything. When we went to Jason's he'd go straight on the space invaders and he'd be winning in no time. I remember when Ken beat the highest score on the machine and then beat it two more times as well. They were talking about slinging him out. He seemed to have a talent for anything competitive.

I played snooker in Jason's as well but wasn't up to Ken's standard. In fairness, not many others were either. I remember one Saturday-morning tournament. I had to play this guy who I knew would beat me. He was just one of those players I couldn't cope with, who ground it out and wouldn't give you anything. Ken had slept in, as he often did, but I went to wake him up and got him to play the guy instead. He wouldn't have realised he was playing the wrong brother. Well, Ken beat him and we got twenty quid each for it. He had that confidence in his ability even then.

When he was a young boy he had to stand on a biscuit tin to reach the balls. It looked comical but it's how he learned and everyone soon got used to it. He was only a kid but was starting to win money in tournaments. He'd come home and wake up our mother by waving the notes in her face. She'd smile and put the money under her pillow, then go back to sleep.

I was just a club player, nothing special. My highest break was 78 but I earned a few quid here and there by playing some money matches with anyone who was about. I would play Ken quite a bit but there came a time when that stopped because he was obviously a much better player and he wound me up when he beat me. It felt like he was enjoying destroying me just a little too much. He'd be stood there smiling at me and there were times when I wanted to run after him, put my hands around his throat and squeeze the air out of him. On reflection, I'm amazed it didn't actually happen because sometimes he really got to me.

As I saw it he didn't just beat me, he'd humiliate me. There was another snooker hall in Ranelagh called Nat's, which had smaller tables. One time Ken suggested we play a best of five but he didn't even take his coat off to play me, he was so confident he'd win. That felt even more humiliating to me. He was stood there chewing a wine gum, his hood pulled up over his head, potting everything. I couldn't take it and I launched a cue at him. Thankfully, it didn't make proper contact. It caught his shoulder and flew into the wall. It made me feel terrible afterwards because I realised I could have really injured him, but that's how we were back then: it was brotherly love but also brotherly hate. I'm happy to say our relationship has improved quite dramatically since we became adults.

After that incident I pretty much stopped playing Ken because I didn't want any repeat of what happened. But I enjoyed watching him play and it was obvious to me he could do seriously well out of snooker. Sure enough, he rose through the ranks and was successful at every level. I was happy enough for him that he was going to live in London when he turned professional, although the family worried because we'd heard various reports about the area he was living in. Despite the way we'd fought as kids I missed him terribly. The only time we'd see him for months at a time was on the TV.

The first time he played on TV was against Eddie Charlton. We were all still living at home at the time and so we gathered round to watch him. It was an unbelievable moment, quite surreal really because there was our Ken, actually on the television playing snooker. We were so proud and thinking, if only our dad could be here to see him. It was a bittersweet moment but it proved that all his hard work and sacrifices had paid off.

I don't go to see him play much because you don't want to take up too much of his time. He's got to concentrate on what he's doing and you don't want to mess with that. Also, there was a time when people would ring me looking for tickets for his matches and I didn't like that because it was more hassle for him. But I enjoy going to his exhibitions, particularly the ones with Jimmy White, because they're more relaxed. My only regret is that I didn't go to the Crucible in 1997 when he won the world title. I would have loved to have shared in that.

Ken has made us all proud. There have been big matches that have gone against him but, then again, he would admit there have been times where he's been lazy, not practising enough and maybe he lost the odd final because of that. I think he could have done better but he's done better than most and I think he's achieved most of his goals. He's always

231

been mentally strong which is why he's done well in the biggest tournaments.

Ken hasn't changed. He's still the same down-to-earth lad he always was. His family and friends wouldn't let him change. I think we've kept him grounded because we've never treated him any differently, despite his success. He's never played the star or tried to act the big man. His fame isn't something he's traded on. Our mother brought all of us up to respect people regardless of who they are or where they've come from. I've seen other players behaving badly, expecting people to do everything for them and it's rather sad to witness.

My brother has never been like that and I'm happy to say that we have long since got over our differences. Put it this way: I no longer want to kill him.

ROSEMARIE (sister)

I'm two years younger than Ken, so I'm the youngest of all the four siblings. Our eldest brother, Seamus, was so much older than us and very settled, whereas Anthony was a little wilder. I think he had that middle-child syndrome of the three brothers but Anthony and Ken are like chalk and cheese in terms of personality, so Ken was never going to get mixed up in trouble with him. He's very strong-willed and always goes his own way. If he hadn't been like that his whole life might have turned out differently, because he needed to put in all the hours of practising and properly dedicate himself to snooker.

I'd love to be able to report some dirt or scandal but the truth is that Ken was well behaved as a boy and was always out, either playing football or snooker. He was a happy child but competitive as well. Whatever we played as kids, even if it was just snakes and ladders, he would want to win. It was never enough just to play for the fun of it – he had that competitive spirit even then. He has this laid-back persona but inside he is very determined. If he sets his mind to something he usually does it.

We got on pretty well as kids, especially between the ages of 9 and 11, probably because we were the two youngest. We'd go swimming together on a Saturday evening, when Ken would always pick up a gold medal, and to summer school. He'd tease me and my friends, steal our dolls, that sort of thing, but that's just normal at that age. He'd get on my nerves but I'm sure I got on his as well.

There was one incident, which he still mentions, when the teasing ended up spilling over into something more serious. Ken had been given a lovely watch for winning the Irish Under-16 title. It had a snooker player on the face and a black strap – I can still picture it to this day. It was Ken's pride and joy because it was his first real man's watch and he'd won it playing snooker. We'd been fighting about something and he went into my bedroom, took my clothes from my wardrobe and dumped them all on the landing. Of course I went mad, so I took his watch because I knew it was his most treasured possession, maybe after his cue, and threw it at the wall. It broke into pieces, the springs bouncing on the floor.

Ken wanted to kill me and it took him ages to forgive me. He still brings it up to this day, although we laugh about it now. That was the first time my mum smacked me because even though I'm the youngest, Ken is really her little pet.

She's always doted on him and she knew what the watch meant to him.

I didn't take much notice of Ken's snooker or think that it could be a career for him. Our mother didn't like him playing so much, and there'd be arguments about it, but they were boys and they did their thing while I had my own friends and my own interests. Then as he got older, he started winning more and more and it became obvious he had a talent for the game. That's when we'd go and watch him.

When Ken finished school he told Mum he wanted to go to England to pursue his snooker career. She was very worried about him, where he was staying, what the area was like and whether he'd be all right. But I think she knew she couldn't stop him doing what he wanted to do with his life. I went over a couple of times with Mum to spend some time with him. He seemed to be enjoying himself and eventually got an apartment, which pleased her because she knew he was settled then. He had some good friends around him, including older guys who looked after him.

We'd always watch him on the TV in the early days and I used to love going to Goffs for the Irish Masters because there was such a great atmosphere, but I found it difficult to relax because I wanted him to win so much. The tension really gets to you, more than you'd imagine, when you're watching your own brother playing snooker. It made it hard to enjoy the matches.

I've been proud of his achievements, none more than when he won the World Championship, but I couldn't believe my eyes when I read all the newspaper stories about Ken being thrown off the plane in Malta. It would have been totally out of character and I had to field a few comments at work about it, but in some ways it did him a favour because a lot of people don't want to look at someone like Ken and think he's just saintly. He didn't really do anything wrong but it probably didn't harm his image in any case, even if it did embarrass him. I didn't recognise my brother from some of the reports. He was never one to get in trouble, not even at school.

I felt for Ken when his form started to go a couple of years ago and he went through a really bad run of results. He got very down on himself because he didn't know where his career was going. I'd try and stay positive for him and tell him that there would always be another tournament, but it's hard to know what to say when you've not been in that position yourself. Your priorities change as well when you get older. Ken has a young son now and he can't just concentrate on snooker because he has other responsibilities and demands on his time.

Even though he's had low moments, at least he's spent his life doing something he's loved, which not everybody can say. I think he'll stay involved with snooker. He's doing TV work now and he enjoys that, and whatever happens to him in the future he's well respected for his contribution to snooker and as an ambassador for Ireland. He put in a table at his old school and does work for charities, so he has put something back and it means people look up to him. I'm proud of him for that.

We're still a very close family but I don't see all that much of Ken these days because we have our own lives and he's away quite a bit at tournaments. We do get together every now and again, for birthdays, weddings, that type of thing, and he hasn't changed. He's still Ken and he's still a messer. He's like a big kid, playing little jokes and messing around but he's not got big-headed or been seduced by the limelight. He's still my brother.

SARAH (wife)

When I first met Ken I had no idea who he was. The only sport I followed was cricket but I knew nothing about snooker.

I was in a bar with a very good friend of mine. We'd been studying for our psychiatry exams and we were out letting our hair down afterwards. Ken was there with a bunch of his friends. He made some comment at the bar about me needing a stepladder to be served and I thought it was a pretty stupid remark, but of course I didn't know him or his sense of humour at that point.

We were sat next to his group of friends and as the evening wore on we got talking. It wasn't love at first sight – we were just chatting – but afterwards we all went out to Lillie's, a club. He was good fun but it didn't enter my head then that this would be the man I'd marry. It was all very relaxed and good natured. I was heading home and Ken mentioned he was going the same way, so I gave him a lift and he asked for my phone number. I wouldn't say I was sat at home waiting for him to call but a couple of days later he did and we slowly started meeting. It was a gradual thing, starting off with an easygoing friendship because he was good company and easy to talk to.

I didn't understand snooker. I knew a little about pool and had heard that snooker was a more complicated game but I had no idea of the skill that was required. I found it interesting that Ken was a snooker player – it was a little bit different. His profession actually suited me because I was busy myself with my internship, and the fact that he was away so much gave me time to focus on that. It suited him as well because I wasn't some needy girlfriend counting down the days until he came back.

One of the main things I liked about Ken, which was different to some of the other lads I'd dated, was that he was very unassuming and humble, and he was straightforward. What you saw was what you got. There were no silly games and all the nonsense you sometimes get in relationships, although we had our ups and downs as well while we were going out. We're quite independent people and so I have a lot of friends and a demanding job just as Ken does. Things have changed a little since we had Christian. Ken finds it much more difficult to be away from his son but has to balance that against the demands of his career, which I know he finds tough.

I'd come over to Ireland from Australia to study and the plan was always to return home but I've settled down with Ken in Dublin. My parents always liked him but I think they thought I'd maybe marry someone from an established profession like a doctor or a lawyer and come back home and live my life there. My parents are very traditional and Ken, a snooker player, represented everything they thought I wouldn't become involved with: he has a career which is relatively short and playing snooker doesn't really sound like a job when you don't understand the sport. Even to this day they don't get what being a snooker player entails but they do like him. Their only regret is that I'm here in Ireland, particularly now they have a grandchild.

I obviously knew that there was no way Ken could be based in Australia given his career, but it only really hit me that I'd be so far from home when we got married and that did cause a bit of difficulty early on for us. But then I went home for a year for work and although it was hard to be apart, it was one of the best things I could have done because at the end of it I realised that I'd been missing Ireland and that maybe it wasn't so bad after all. I'd got living back in Australia out of my system and I regard Dublin as my home now.

I've come to like snooker. It's a fascinating game and extremely skilful but I don't want to spend any time at tournaments. I've been to a few exhibitions because they are more fun but I don't have the time to spend sitting around backstage and Ken has never asked me to go. He needs his own space and routines in any case. He doesn't come to my work and I don't go to his.

When Ken loses he does tend to sulk around the house for a couple of days and I just leave him to it. The 2008/09 season was a nightmare for him: he was losing all the time and couldn't qualify for anything. That was a terrible time. He was constantly sulking and I couldn't get a conversation out of him for the best part of a year. That was quite a difficult time in the relationship and I think we drifted apart as a result. Christian was born during that period and Ken had to adjust to becoming a father at the same time as his career was going downhill. It was hard because he was going off to qualifiers and losing and at the same time missing out on his son's early months. He's away a lot more now with his BBC work and all the new events he's playing in, and it's tough for both of us to strike the balance between work and family.

I try to use what I've learned in my job to help Ken when he comes home from a tournament if he's not done too well, but I find it hard to remove the emotional aspect of our relationship from giving him advice. I'm part of it so it's hard to be professional, as I would be with anyone else. To see your own husband low – often amazingly low – for periods rather than the usual happy-go-lucky Ken affects you as well. If Ken is nervous about a tournament I will try and give him advice but you can be too close. You lose your objectivity when you're married to someone.

After he qualified for the World Championship in 2010 things turned around a little because it gave him back some of his lost confidence and persuaded him that he might not be finished after all. Ken is defined as being a snooker player and it's hard for him to have to face the fact that he might not be playing snooker for much longer. It affects every other aspect of his life as well.

I'm seeing a different side to Ken now that he's a father. He's devoted to Christian, although he's not a great disciplinarian. I think he feels that as he's away so much, he has to make it up to Christian when he's at home in case he loses a bit of love. So I'm left to be the strict one while Ken does all the cool things, taking him out and bringing him lollipops and so on. Being a father has been good for him, though. He's developed a bit more purpose and has more structure to his day. I'd always go out working early while Ken would be lying in bed. A lot of people have said he's lazy and it's probably true that all his life he's had people doing things for him, but now he gets up early because if he doesn't he thinks he's missing out on time with Christian. He's more organised now and he's spending far more time at home. He's let a few of the crowd around him drop into the background and is concentrating on his closer friends and his family.

There's no doubt that his sense of family comes from his mother, who has grounded him in a very particular set of values. She has raised him to be respectful, kind and considerate. The time he got chucked off the plane in Malta Ken was very worried about how both his mum and I would react, because I'm from a conservative background too. I don't drink or smoke, and I think I'm therefore a little like Rose in that respect. I was surprised and disappointed when it happened. It was completely out of character. I've never seen him aggressive so it was shocking to hear about what happened, although Ken says it was all blown out of proportion and that it was John Higgins who was drunk. But it was so public and it felt like everyone knew. I was so embarrassed going into work the following day.

Ireland is a pretty laid-back place and they don't really bother Ken. There's the odd time when that changes, like at a party when someone's had a drink and they're uninhibited and all over Ken. In that situation it's a bit like the Prince Charles syndrome for me; I'm just hanging around like a spare part. Usually people are very polite. When we're walking the dogs people do come up to Ken but it's always in a friendly way.

There's been the odd stupid remark from young lads but it's obvious from what people say to him that Ken is well liked by the public.

Ken isn't going to go on playing forever but he's been doing broadcasting work for the BBC and on radio in Ireland and he's realised that he can't always define himself as a snooker player. He's looking forward to his future when he stops playing and that's healthy because it means he's being realistic. He enjoys the broadcasting and he comes over naturally, so I think that's going to play a large part in his future. When he does hang up his cue I believe the transition will be relatively easy for him.

He's taken most things in his stride and seems to be contented with what he's done in his chosen career. I don't think there are many things he would change and it's not everyone who can say that.

PAT CAULFIELD (coach and circuit companion)

I've known Ken since he was 13. I used to drive him to all the amateur tournaments with a couple of other guys, one of whom was a bookie. We'd have bets on Ken and if they came in we'd have money for food and drink. It was great craic, good fun. It wasn't about money but the enjoyment of going around playing snooker, having a few bets and a laugh.

I saw Ken's potential right away. It was obvious to anyone who understood the game. I managed to get Ken some sponsorship when he went to England because when you have money worries it's hard to focus on playing but he won his first event, the Open at Pontins, and got something like three grand for that, so he was able to go his own way. When he first tried to turn professional through the Pro Ticket route we applied for a government grant for him and on the form you had to write why the player was deserving of it. I wrote that I thought Ken would be world champion. Even as a kid he had something that you don't see very often. He was a talented player and very good under pressure. What impressed me most was that he was so clever and he brought that to his snooker. He doesn't make hasty decisions: he considers what he's doing and usually plays the right shot. He uses his experience and the knowledge he's gained since he started playing.

Although I've given Ken support over the years, he would have been world champion regardless of who was in his corner because he was always driven, ambitious and determined to succeed. He'd proved that as an amateur when he won all there was to win. He believed in himself and confidence makes such a difference in any sport, particularly in snooker which requires much more mental than physical energy.

Ken's main fault over the years is that he hasn't always been the most hard-working. Sometimes I've had to drag him out of bed to practise but more recently he's been much better, because he's slipped down the rankings and wants to get back up. In fairness to Ken he would always work hard when he put his mind to it and would seek out matches and tournaments wherever they were played. He sometimes just needed a bit of a jolt to get him going.

Most of my work is done before we go to tournaments,

working with Ken on the practice table. I probably know Ken's game better than anyone and I've learned over the years how to talk to him, what to say and what advice to give. You're basically trying to give them a bit of belief, build them up and reassure them that a couple of disappointing results doesn't suddenly make them a bad player. So we've put the work in before we get to a tournament and then when we get there I just try and keep his head right, keep him happy and also keep him company. There's a lot of time at tournaments like the World Championship where you're not playing and that's dangerous, because there's time to become worked up about a match or a session. So we'll take a walk or go to the cinema or do anything to take away the natural pressure that the player is feeling. It's all about staying positive.

Snooker can be an unforgiving game. One mistake and you can be heavily punished. Also, you're out there on your own with no one to help you. Even the strongest characters in the sport have times when they feel down, like nothing is going right for them. I can tell when Ken is nervous so I try and help him by maybe setting up easier shots on the practice table than normal. Instead of getting him to pot long balls, we'd work on short-range pots. That hopefully helps to get his confidence back.

After coming back from a tournament after a defeat we wouldn't talk for a couple of days. You need to give the player a bit of space to get over losing. After that we might speak about what happened but there's no point in dwelling on it too much. We might talk about whether the tactics were right but I wouldn't overdo it. You can't tell a player that he's played the wrong shot because they are the ones who are down there and they feel in the moment what's right and wrong. They have to be comfortable with those choices.

It's important not to celebrate too much when things go right. You don't learn by winning, you learn by making mistakes. You have to look to the next tournament and not dwell on the last one too much, whether you've won it or not.

I'll never forget being at the Crucible in 1997 when Ken won the World Championship. It was the icing on the cake for all of his supporters after following him for so many years from the junior days through the amateur ranks and in his early years as a professional. When the final finished, I rushed out into the arena and whispered in his ear to just enjoy the moment because he'd reached the pinnacle of the sport. A snooker player can't do anything better than become world champion. The tournament is a tough road, 17 days of toil. You have to get through the first week and then build up your game and you need stamina just to make it to the last day. You also have to be able to shut out all the pressure around you and the demands on your time from the media and everyone else.

Coming back to Ireland was incredible. The reception was like nothing I'd ever seen before. Ken was well liked at the time because he doesn't know how to say no to anybody. If people want a slice of him he's usually there, which is a sort of kindness he's probably inherited from his mother. Because of this he had so many friends and well wishers by 1997 that a huge part of the country was genuinely delighted for him when he came back with the trophy. A lot of them had met him, liked him and felt they knew him. He was one of them and they were able to share in his success.

I remember a few years ago in the Dáil, our governing house, there was a debate about the state of the country's finances. This was just after Ken had beaten Paul Hunter 17-16 from 15-9 down in the World Championship semi-finals. The politicians were trading figures and one of the ministers stood up and said, 'I don't know where you're getting your figures from but even Ken Doherty wouldn't come back from that.' That shows you how well known he is.

I didn't believe Stephen Hendry would ever beat Ken in that final. I could sense it, even though Hendry was obviously a great player who had won the title the five previous years. Ken was on fire; he had so much belief in himself over the course of those three weeks.

I think Ken had a great chance to win the title when he was in the final again in 1998 against John Higgins. They were like two boxers in the middle of the ring but Higgins was the player scoring heavily. I told Ken he needed to tie the game up more, make 40 and hide the cue ball rather than taking Higgins on in the break-building game, but he kept playing the same way and it cost him. I think if he'd played the clever game that he knows inside out he could have beaten Higgins but pride took over and, like a couple of boxers, each wanted to land the biggest punch.

In 2003, he was in the final again. He came from 11-5 down to 12-12 with Mark Williams and then there was a break between sessions, which I think was the key part of the match. Williams had only won one frame in that third session. It was all Ken. But because they had to stop, it gave Williams a chance to regroup and stopped Ken's momentum. In the final session, Williams seemed to have decided just to go for everything and if they went in he'd win, if not the title would be Ken's. Fair play to him, he potted them off the lampshades and he won 18-16. To get to three world finals was a great achievement but I always thought Ken would win at least two titles. It just wasn't to be.

Ken has never forgotten his role as an ambassador, not just for snooker but for Ireland as well. After he lost to Higgins in the 1998 world final we were about to be driven back to the hotel by John Carroll from 110sport. This kid ran across the road just as we were about to pull away and banged on the door. Ken opened it, signed an autograph and posed for a photo. This was just an hour or so after losing his world title. It would have left a great impression on that kid and at the same time presented a positive image of snooker. He's been well grounded by his mother and, like her, would not do any harm to anyone or want to see any harm done to them. She's a huge influence on him.

I suppose our relationship is a little like father and son because I'm that much older than Ken and we talk through everything together, not just snooker. I've followed his progress with great pride but I'm not surprised by his success. He was always destined for great things in my eyes.

MARTIN COSGRAVE AND TOM KEARNEY (Jason's)

MARTIN: My father and uncle ran Jason's and another uncle owned it. Jack Cosgrave originally bought the building but couldn't decide what to do with it, so in the meantime he put a pool hall in there. My father ran it in the 1970s and then in the 1980s snooker exploded on colour television. By then my uncle Derry was running the club. He was a character; he kept going bankrupt and bouncing back. He had a varied past: he was the first man to introduce barbecued chicken to Ireland in the 1960s and he had the first microwave in Ireland. He was one of those people who could spot trends and see what was popular, and snooker is an example of that. He pushed Jason's from pool to snooker. Jason's eventually had 26 full-sized snooker tables having had just one, which was lit by sunlight shining through the windows.

Ken and his brothers would come in and play pinball and table football more than pool or snooker at the beginning. There were a lot of lads who started playing snooker and reached a certain level but couldn't improve on it, but Ken was someone who just got better and better.

He spent a lot of time in Jason's – too much for his mother, who would come in with her wooden spoon, chasing Ken round the club. He was small so he could get under the table and then out of the door and she'd be waving her spoon at us for letting him in when he should have been doing his homework.

TOM: Ken was in Jason's any chance he got. Jason's was unique. There was a magic about the place and it attracted all the kids in the area. Ireland was quite a depressed place at the time but Jason's was a happy environment, somewhere to go and enjoy yourself.

Ken was always polite, never shy. He was good at school

and loved his football. There was always a competition to play in at Jason's itself every Saturday. The players were having to give Ken a start per frame, which many of them didn't like. It was a kind of handicap system used whereby nobody won twice in a row. Everyone got a chance to win something, which boosted their confidence.

There was never any jealousy towards Ken from the other players because he'd grown up in Jason's and they all knew and liked him. He wasn't necessarily the best player in the club as a teenager but he was the one who went on to enjoy most success. Some players drifted away a bit through work, took to other sports or to drink, but Ken kept on playing and got the rewards.

In the mid-1980s, Gay Byrne was the Irish champion and was winning everything, a bit like Steve Davis was doing in the professional ranks. Paddy Miley was coaching Ken and was a bit like Cliff Thorburn in that he had the tactical know-how, which he passed on to Ken. That's when people started to sit up and take notice of him. He was starting to win so many tournaments that it all snowballed and he went on to win the world amateur title.

MARTIN: After that he went to England to pursue a professional career. We'd miss him around the club because he'd become a permanent fixture, but we wished him well and we knew it was only a matter of time before we'd see him on the TV. He'd be in the newspapers every now and then, little reports of his progress, and he was always destined to have his name in lights. I think we all believed he'd get there.

TOM: We followed his progress pretty closely. In the early days Martin and myself went over to the UK for an exhibition in London. Ken was playing at Wembley in the Masters and got me a VIP badge, but when we went into the arena the security guard stopped him because he wasn't wearing one. Ken tried to explain that he was a player but the guard didn't recognise him because he hadn't been on the circuit that long and he hadn't become established. Eventually I had to vouch for him because I was the one with the badge.

MARTIN: We didn't have a television set in the club but when Ken got to the World Championship final in 1997 we knew we'd have to get one because everyone would want to see it. On the first day of the final I bought two TVs. We didn't have cabling or a TV licence but we managed to rig them up and of course people poured in to watch. On the second day of the final I got two more TVs. By now we had TV news crews down, reporters and cameramen, going live from Jason's and there we were sponging off cabling from somewhere else and no licence for the TVs.

The homecoming for Ken was unbelievable. The welcome he got was incredible and the party went on and on. The people of Ranelagh wanted to show their appreciation for what he'd done and celebrate the fact that he was one of them, that he'd learned his trade in their community. Everyone was genuinely happy for him and joined in. We'd already started building a private room for him to practise in because he was moving back from Ilford. He put his own table in there so he could concentrate on practising without being bothered, because people had started to come to the club after he became world champion. Such was the fame of Jason's by then.

TOM: We had a wall with pictures of Ken on it and from that day we'd have strangers calling in to see the place where Ken Doherty played snooker. People would have their photographs taken there. Every year the local school would come down to do a tour of Jason's because of Ken.

He also challenged people's preconceptions of what snooker clubs were like. They might look at someone like Alex Higgins and think that clubs were a den of iniquity, but Ken was more personable, more presentable, and you'd look at him and think, 'I'd quite like my son to get involved in snooker.' That certainly helped Jason's.

We'd get so many regular faces even if, like Ken, they went away for a time. People had spent their childhoods in there then may have moved away, but whenever they came back they popped in to Jason's to relive old memories. We'd look up and say, 'Where have you been?' We'd have famous people as well. One day a guy came in saying he had a soccer team over and could they come in for a few frames of snooker? We said no problem. Next thing, the Tottenham Hotspur team, including Paul Gascoigne and Gary Lineker, was in our club.

MARTIN: I remember they went into the newsagent's next door to Jason's, which we also owned. There was a stand of footballs and some of the players started heading them. Jack

Cosgrave, the owner, called over to them, 'Now lads, put the balls down or get out!'

TOM: We had some fun at Jason's and Ken was usually part of that. When he was in the Masters final against Matthew Stevens, Jason's was packed with people glued to the television. He had that black for a 147 and the expensive car that came with it but missed. A couple of weeks later he was back in the club and there was a rugby match on featuring Ireland. One of the players missed a kick and Ken couldn't believe it. He turned to someone and said, 'How the hell did he miss that?' and this young lad piped up, 'We all said the same two weeks ago when you missed that black.' It was always good humoured. It wasn't the sort of club where you could get ahead of yourself. If you did, you'd soon be put in your place.

Ken had a great attitude and he wouldn't come in the club sulking if he'd just lost in a tournament. He'd be more likely to make a joke of it. He might tell you what happened, that he shouldn't have gone for a certain ball or that the other guy had a bit of luck at the right time, but he wouldn't go on about it. He'd try and learn from his mistakes rather than dwell too much on them.

MARTIN: Jason's closed in 2005. It was doing great business but in Ireland at that time people had got greedy. Property prices and rents were too high. The owners thought they could get much more for it than was the reality. It's been locked up since the day we closed the door, just lying empty. Someone came up to me in the street and said that Jason's closing was like someone dying. The people had nowhere to go. We were popular with night workers, taxi drivers and so on, not big drinkers by any means, just people who wanted to come in, have a cup of tea and a chat, maybe a game of snooker and to generally relax. Ken never forgot where he came from and would always give us a mention in the media. It put Jason's on the map, made it the centre of the community. When it shut down it was a big loss to that community but we're proud of the role it played in Ken's career and of what he went on to do with the talent he nurtured there.

PADDY MILEY (coach)

When I first met Ken he was 13. I used to run handicap tournaments in Jason's on Saturday and Sunday mornings and he'd be one of the 15 to 20 lads who would play in it. Ken lived the nearest to Jason's of any of them but would always be the last to arrive because he struggled to get out of bed. He progressed pretty quickly and I started coaching him. He was winning these tournaments so we started entering him in the Under-14s, Under-16s and Under-18s events played around Ireland. There was a time when I'd give him 35 start per frame but I'd be looking for double that now from him if we played these days.

Ken was one of a group of players who stood out. He was dedicated and listened to advice about how to play the game. He developed more quickly than some of the other lads and played a mature game from a young age. I tried to instil in Ken the importance of playing the right shot but when he was a lad he understandably didn't always know what it was. He was playing in one junior tournament and I told him I'd cough when he was lining up a ball to let him know if it was the right shot. The way he did it, nobody would have known. He looked at one ball, I coughed, he'd then go and look at another ball as if he was still thinking about which one to play. Then he returned to the first ball and potted it. It was one way that he learned about tactics.

He would have a fear as a kid of playing certain players because he felt they played a superior game, but I tried to show him he had to face up to them and the way he could erase his fears was to play them and beat them. As soon as he did that all the fear was gone, because he knew he could match them. We were playing in the Dublin league one time and he was drawn against Jimmy Long from Dun Laoghaire, who Ken didn't want to play. He said, 'You play him,' but that wasn't the way to learn.

Ken loved his snooker but he was also very much into football and his family wanted to know which, if either, he should pursue. I remember meeting his mother and brother, Seamus, and they asked me if he had the potential to be a successful snooker player. I said I had no doubt that he did but that it was up to Ken. I stressed that he had the right temperament for snooker because he never gave up and although I think his mother was wary of snooker, it seemed to reassure them.

They let me take Ken to tournaments in Tralee or Cork or wherever they were on. He had to play in these events because you only improve by playing regular match snooker. By the time he was about 17 it became clear that he would have to go to England because he was beating everyone in Ireland and he needed still better opposition. In Ireland he could afford three or four mistakes a frame and still win it but over in the UK one mistake could cost you and he needed to expose himself to that.

I knew Eugene Hughes, who was living in England, and he offered to put Ken up, but his mother wasn't happy about him going away. I just tried to tell her that it was the only way he could be successful, like a footballer playing here for a team like Shamrock Rovers. That's fine but to be the best you have to make it with Manchester United or Liverpool, and Ken wanted to reach the top. He had that determination to get there.

And he did get there. I couldn't be more proud to have witnessed his success, particularly when he won the world title. I think he could have won it again in 2003. He rang me on the first day of the final against Mark Williams, which he ended 11-5 down, and asked me to come over. I told him what I thought he was doing wrong: Williams is a left-handed player so get him over the other side of the table, get the cue ball on the back cushion so he can't get his hand on the table, and when you get to 50 or 60 run the white back to the cushion and give him nothing. He came back to 12-12 and after that the match was anyone's. It proved what a good fighter Ken was, even though he ultimately came up short in the final.

When he was young he would get frustrated but I would try and make him forget about a ball he had just missed and concentrate on what was ahead of him. I always reminded the lads that snooker is a game in which they are in control when at the table. Your opponent is in his seat so what you must do is make it as difficult as you can for the other guy when he does eventually get his chance. One of the ways to improve is to practise the shots you're weak on. It's all very well making a big break but you also need to use your brain in the tactical department.

Ken was educated and behaved properly, but he would also be one of the lads who enjoyed a few drinks. He has always had a very easy way of talking to people and is well liked in Ireland. There's not really any jealousy about his success, none that I've encountered anyway. Part of the reason for that is that he hasn't changed or treated people differently since becoming a big name. He has always been humble and that's one of the reasons he would listen to advice because he didn't think, like some young players, that he knew it all already. His life has changed and he has a lovely family of his own now but snooker is still in his blood and I hope he plays for as long as he wants to.

FINBAR RUANE (friend)

I first met Ken playing in a junior tournament at the Classic Snooker Club. There was a Saturday morning league we began playing in, which is how we got to know each other. We were both picked for the Irish Home Internationals team in 1984 and have been good pals ever since.

I was working in America when Ken went to live in England with Stephen Murphy and Anthony O'Connor to pursue their snooker careers. I'd stopped playing seriously by then but decided I would follow them over. I based myself in King's Cross where I managed a pub. We decided to live together and got a house in Chadwell Heath: Ken, Steven, Damien McKiernan and myself. We'd called ourselves 'Birds of a Feather' after the TV sitcom, which was set in Essex. I'd go off to work in the morning, the boys would go and practise in Ilford and that was the daily routine. If we had any money left after rent and shopping, we'd go out for a few pints in an Irish bar close by.

This was in the days before mobile phones and email, so staying in touch with our families wasn't as simple as it would be now. We'd make our phone calls back home on a Friday or a Sunday. Ken got homesick quite a bit and would go home every now and then, or his brothers would come over to see him. His mum came over a few times as well. Ken missed home more than anyone. His family has always been close and his mum is like my second mum: she'd do anything for anyone. We kept each other company and we were always laughing and joking about something. Eugene Hughes deserves immense credit. He set the lads up in Ilford and gave them so much support. He helped make it like a home from home when it could have been a lonely experience. We'd have people who would look after us, give us dinner on a Sunday, give us lifts when we needed them. Ronnie O'Sullivan's dad was a prime example of that. He was good as gold to us.

If I'd been paid a bonus or if any of the lads had done well in a tournament we'd treat ourselves. If one of the guys was struggling for a few quid the rest would see them right, Ken more than anyone. One time he won £500 in a Christmas tournament in Ilford. I wasn't going home because even though I could afford the flight I needed the money for other things, but Ken said he'd buy me the ticket. That's what he was like. He'd help someone if they needed it. He's still like that to this day. I've seen people change in snooker, even when they've not done much in the game, but Ken hasn't at all. He's well grounded, which is down to his family. His mother was strict but brought him up to respect people.

He's canny as well, particularly with money. We used to get the 86 bus from Chadwell Heath. We'd joke that times were so tight that if the fare was 45p and Ken had 50p he'd wait for the 5p back. The way he saw it, nine of those was a free journey. He'd keep us on our toes, making sure the rent was paid on time and all the other bills as well. That was all down to him. He'd been the same as a kid. He'd play money matches against older players but would hold his nerve. He was always reliable under pressure.

Ilford was a hotbed of snooker in those days and there'd always be a quality pro-am on a Saturday nearby. You'd be guaranteed a good field, a chance to toughen up your game and decent money if you did well. Back then the pro-am scene in the UK was thriving. I remember one at Willie Thorne's in Leicester. It was my first time seeing one of these pro-ams up close and Ken went through the field and won it. It really impressed me. I knew he'd always been a good player but I could see that he really was ready to take the next step. He didn't gloat on the way home. It was just business and a job well done.

This was just before he lost to Dave Harold in the pro ticket match that cost him a place on the professional circuit. Ken was certainly good enough to have turned pro that year but it wasn't to be and he was absolutely gutted. I've never seen him that disappointed since then. He went back home and I honestly thought he'd even consider chucking snooker and doing something else. He'd done well at school and had qualifications behind him, so he could have gone into a different field. But snooker was his first love and he got his head down, won the Irish amateur title, then won the world amateurs and got on the tour anyway. In hindsight it was the best thing that ever happened to him because it made him even tougher and he proved to himself how much he cared about snooker and how much he wanted to make a go of it.

Ken was the most dedicated of all the group who went over from Ireland to try their luck. Some of the boys didn't like getting up on a Saturday morning for a tournament but Ken never missed one. You could tell he had the right attitude for the game.

In 1993 I started travelling to tournaments with him. I'd taken over my dad's club and I could take time off to go with Ken, which was great fun. Snooker tournaments can be pretty long and it's about how you fill your time when you're not playing. Most evenings there'd be a football match on or we'd go to the movies or for something to eat. It wasn't a glamorous lifestyle of wine, women and song that some people imagine. We'd sit in the hotel room and just talk or watch the TV. Ken wanted to relax away from the pressure of the tournaments.

I was at the Crucible in 1997 when he won the world title. I got to Sheffield on the Wednesday night, the last day of the quarter-finals. There hadn't been that much coverage in the Irish media up to that point but I phoned home on the first day of the final and my folks said it was all over the newspapers. By the last day of the final it was being covered live on RTE in Ireland, which was unheard of. The people of Ireland tapped into it. There wasn't a single call to the main police station in Dublin on the evening Ken won. There was so much interest that there wasn't any crime that night. The reception he got when he returned home was amazing. Suddenly in all the bars we normally went in Ken was being called to the front, no need to queue.

He didn't go mad when he won. I don't think it really sunk in until a couple of weeks after he won when they put a night on for him in Ranelagh with a band and all the locals came out to support him. He got up to say a few words, looked at the trophy, and the emotion of what he'd achieved hit home at that point. He could see that it meant so much to everyone else what he'd done.

He's had his setbacks too but I did my best to try and keep him positive. One thing we'd do is crack jokes in the dressing room so that he went out to play upbeat. He'd walk out of his dressing room laughing while his opponent would be stony-faced. One time at the Crucible the head of security knocked on the door and asked us to keep it down because they could hear us laughing all the way along the corridor.

Ken has won more than most but he's had a lot of runner-up spots too. I think he could have won another world title but it's probably too late now, although he could still win another ranking title. You never know with snooker. Players who have looked like they were on the slide have got it together before, a good example being Steve Davis.

I think when he had to leave Jason's and go and practise in the hotel
he didn't put the same amount of hours in, but becoming a father helped because he's no longer just playing for himself and it's given him a new lease of life. There are more tournaments now and he seems to have got his enthusiasm back. It's easy to see why it went. Snooker was his great passion but it became a job and it isn't the jet-set lifestyle that people think. The reality is acres of time spent in hotels and airports, away from your loved ones. Ken wouldn't complain about that because it's the path he's chosen but having done it for 20 years it's understandable it would become a bit of a grind.

When Ken looks back, he can be proud of his career. There have been matches that could have gone either way, some he could have won but some he could have lost as well. I'm delighted that he's still out there battling away when so many players he grew up with have fallen by the wayside over the years. I still get a buzz when he sends me a text to tell me he's won. I'm happy that he still gets so much enjoyment out of snooker.

IAN DOYLE (former manager)
I first became aware of Ken after he won the world amateur title. I'm friendly with Eamon Dunphy, who is also a pal of

Ken's, and he spoke to me about him and then I went over to Dublin to meet his mum and family.

I always liked to speak to families before I signed a player because while they can be very supportive, they can also be a complete pain. The bottom line was that his family were just lovely people. They made me really welcome and every time I've been to see his mother she's had cake and tea ready for me. She's worked so hard for that family and they're all lovely people.

Ken wasn't any trouble for me. The only problem I ever had with him was that I thought he could have worked harder on occasions. Before the 1997 World Championship I spoke to his mum, because I didn't want her to read it in the papers without knowing anything about it, and I told her I would be having my say, calling him lazy and so on. I was trying to fire him up.

I ripped into him, basically. After he won the title I went to Dublin for the parade through the city streets and at about half-six the next morning I got into a taxi to go to the airport. The driver turned round and said, 'Mr Doyle, you should have kicked his arse years ago. I'm fed up of picking him up outside nightclubs at three in the morning.' I just burst out laughing.

It had been difficult for me to criticise one of my own players so publicly like that. It wasn't a spur of the moment thing. I just felt he had more in him and he wasn't doing himself full justice. I wasn't sure how he'd respond to it but he won the world title and I was very proud of him. My only disappointment is that he didn't win it again. I think he was better than a one-time winner.

261

Of course Ken played another of my stable, Stephen Hendry, in the final. I tried to stay independent and keep away from them, other than wishing them both luck.

The only other problem with Ken, and this has been a trait of other Irish people I've worked with, is that he has got himself involved in other things away from the table. In his case it was property. He got involved in buying property and I couldn't keep up with how much he'd bought. Maybe that took an edge off his concentration and his game.

How much longer Ken carries on depends on his attitude. I'd like to see him climbing the rankings again. I know he still loves the game so there's no need to retire as long as he stays like that. It's always up to the player to decide. I couldn't tell him when the right time to stop would be.

Steve Davis is a bit of a one-off. Steve is so much in love with the game that he'll keep playing as long as he's on the circuit. Hendry has won so much, he's been there and done it and it's hard to keep that focus, particularly in much smaller events, and there are more of those around now.

Ken comes across very well on television and he won't have any problems after his playing days are over. He can have a career in the media but I'm sure he still thinks of himself as a player first and I hope that he can continue to enjoy playing.

PHIL YATES (snooker correspondent of *The Times* and *Irish Independent*)
I would describe Ken Doherty as a friend, and one I'm privileged to have. Indeed, I'm far from alone. Other members of the press have the same relationship with him, even though

older hands in the profession would tell you that writers and commentators should steer well clear of becoming too close to any current sportsmen for fear that it may impair their ability to be objective. But Ken is a true friend to the press in general and a shining example to all of those, whether in snooker or other professional sports, who wilfully shirk their wider responsibilities to be a role model. Much like snooker's other golden media assets such as Steve Davis and John Parrott, Ken has been priceless.

There are those who use the media to shamelessly and repeatedly promote themselves, but Steve, John and Ken promote the game, and do an outstanding job. For that alone, their fellow professionals owe them a debt of gratitude. But Ken's warmth is not only felt by the hacks who inhabit the press room. He is immensely popular, and rightly so, with snooker devotees the world over. This is a man with a fan base from Bangkok to Bournemouth and from Shanghai to Sheffield.

Without wishing to express any hint of cultural snobbery, it is also refreshing to engage with a sportsman who, while thoroughly dedicated to his profession, also has the time and inclination to be passionate about interests ranging from Manchester United to cooking to Caravaggio. Ken also loves a good laugh. Quite often you know he's in the room if you hear his chortle, sometimes not far removed from the sound that might emanate from a demented donkey. He listens to and tells jokes with a schoolboy glee and relishes banter of all kinds. He is not immune to anger – and was livid when Northern Ireland's Mark Allen disrespected and abused the referee in one of their meetings – but his usually placid exterior is not a front. Ken is a fierce competitor but not a fearsome person.

A few days before the 1997 World Championship that would define Ken's career, I contacted his then manager, Ian Doyle, for his views on his Crucible chances. Ian was always a willing supplier of good stories and a reliable quote-smith but what emerged was entirely unexpected, even by his standards. The self-confessed Scottish workaholic launched into a withering attack on his client, insisting that Ken was lazy, did not practise enough and famously 'could sleep for Ireland'. There was no doubt Ken enjoyed a good kip but such criticism was both unwarranted and untimely.

Back then, Doyle was totally wrapped up in snooker. He once confided to me that at five o'clock one morning he annoyed his late wife Irene by using his bedside telephone to ring Bangkok in order to find out the latest Thailand Masters results. No, not for the final, but the wild card play-off round. Doyle was so intense he made Margaret Thatcher, who famously slept just four hours a night, appear something of a slacker.

Needless to say Doyle's 'verbal blast' inspired a substantial eve-of-championship story in Ireland's biggest selling newspaper, the *Irish Independent*. It was an article that carried my by-line and one that I feared would seriously damage my relationship with Ken. Instead, unlike so many others, the recipient of the stick did not blame the messenger. He successfully channelled the hurt and anger from being wrongly labelled a layabout and 17 days later lifted the World Championship trophy.

To this day Doyle insists the whole barrage was nothing more than a motivational tactic designed to stir a sleeping giant. Whatever, Ken's reaction to a piece that might easily have resulted in national ridicule could hardly have been more perceptive or professional. I was not blamed, even though Ken was seething. I was hugely relieved; Ken was determined to prove a point as never before.

Four years later, in 2001, Ken's considerate nature again shone through after one of the most disappointing defeats of his career. Having won the Welsh Open and Thailand Masters, he arrived in Aberdeen for the Scottish Open intent on emulating Steve Davis and Stephen Hendry by triumphing in three successive world-ranking tournaments.

In the Granite City, Ken was snooker granite until he lost 9-7 to Peter Ebdon in a final that had little aesthetic merit. Ludicrously, almost to the point of delusional, Ebdon had the temerity to say that it was a tough match to win because Doherty had slowed him down. The assembled press fully expected a response with a degree of vitriol. Not a chance. Ken just smiled at Ebdon's preposterous comment and said, 'If that's what Peter thinks, let him think it.'

Years later I asked him why he didn't have a go. 'I know what Peter said was utter rubbish but I didn't want a row story to detract from what he'd just achieved,' explained Ken. Now, a decade on, the pair remain on good terms. That was classy, as was Ken's handling of the bitter disappointment caused by inexplicably botching the final black for a 147 and an £80,000 sports car during his defeat by Matthew Stevens in the 2000 Masters final at Wembley Conference Centre.

The vast majority of sports writers hate to gush, and so do I, but when it comes to Ken the temptation is strong. Following the death of Alex Higgins I found it easy and appropriate to write positive things about the player but not the man. That is not an issue with Ken.

Keenly competitive yet compassionate, ruthless on the table but fun-loving and generous away from the green baize, Ken has always had his personal life balance smack on. As they say, his head has not been turned by fame. He is a source of pride to his mother, his wife, his extended family, his multitude of friends and to the Republic of Ireland in general.

When he does pack away his cue for good, it might not be a bad idea for the Taoiseach to buy him a ticket to London or Washington. No country will ever have a better ambassador.

CHAPTER TWENTY-SEVEN

UPDATE

SUMMER 2011

Keeping a journal of the 2009/10 season proved to be quite a cathartic experience for me because it forced me to reassess my priorities as a snooker player, having fallen so low after so many great years. Looking back, I'm proud of the way I recovered and started to climb the rankings again.

We've had another season since then. From my point of view it started pretty promisingly but tailed off towards the end. However, I kept my top 32 place, ending the campaign in 29th position, and certainly didn't go backwards. It was just disappointing that the season petered out for me. I was 6-3 up after the first session of my final qualifying round match against Jimmy Robertson in the World Championship but didn't win another frame. I don't know what happened, really, other than that I started to miss a few and he got a bit of confidence going. To lose 10-6 having been ahead was a sickener and it meant I went to the Crucible only as a BBC pundit rather than as a player.

That result impacted on my performance at the China Open in Beijing, for which I had played well to qualify. I lost out there 5-1 to Li Hang, a local Chinese wildcard, and just felt completely flat throughout the match. It was just a week or so after I'd lost in the World Championship and I was still disappointed. When you don't have the Crucible to look forward to, it affects your entire mindset. I was poor in the match and it wasn't a nice way to end the season.

The good news, though, is that snooker really took off during the year. Earlier in this book I wrote about Barry Hearn and how he should be backed to bring about the changes that need to be made to make snooker more successful. What he's actually done is amazing. We've gone from six ranking tournaments to 20. Of these, 12 have been small Players Tour Championship events, but they still carry points. I played in most of them. The six European ones have the potential to grow but I'm not sure many players enjoyed the six UK ones in Sheffield, which were played in small rooms with no space for any spectators. It may be a better idea to have six bigger PTC events rather than 12 but either way it's more snooker for us to play and that can only be a good thing.

The big disappointment for me was not qualifying for the Grand Finals because they were staged in Dublin. I had helped bring them to Ireland so to not be playing was frustrating.

However, I was still involved as master of ceremonies, which was fun if a bit nerve-racking. The tournament was really well supported, as I knew it would be, by the Irish crowds. Not all the big names qualified but the fans still turned out in force.

Barry has really taken snooker forward and new tournaments are on the calendar in Thailand, Australia and Brazil. It's a really good time to be turning professional and even old hands like me are excited by the changes. After so many years of political rows and off-table distractions the game is now being properly run.

The 2010/11 season culminated with a brilliant Crucible final in which John Higgins won his fourth world title by beating Judd Trump 18-15. This was proof of John's strength of character, to win the World Championship again after his suspension. He also captured the UK Championship and Welsh Open trophies during a remarkable comeback year. Young Judd was a revelation. Just 21, he played some amazing snooker to win the China Open and then followed it up with his run to the final in Sheffield.

His shot-making is like Alex Higgins or Jimmy White at their best and, like them, he will help bring a whole new audience to the sport. He is exactly what the game has been looking for. The atmosphere when he and John were introduced into the Crucible for the final session of the final was like nothing I have ever heard before. It was electrifying. Myself and Willie Thorne were waiting to commentate and neither of us could believe it. Willie was almost in tears. I know he takes some stick from players for his commentaries but he loves the game so much and he was really touched by the reception the two guys got. It proved that snooker has caught fire again and the final was genuinely exciting, which gives the game something to build on.

We didn't hold the Six Reds World Championship during the 2010/11 season but I still own the rights to it. Though it has gone on the back burner for now, I would still like to stage it in the future. There are things I would do differently next time but I still believe it has potential as a tournament. The main problem now is finding gaps in the calendar, with so many new tournaments around.

Another development was the collapse of 110sport, who managed me for almost all my career. Lee Doyle resigned as a board member and a provisional liquidator was appointed just before the 2011 World Championship. I was saddened for Ian Doyle, who built the company up from nothing. In its day it was very successful and we had a lot of fun. It's a shame things developed as they did. I know some of the old 110sport directors are putting together a new stable but I'm not sure I need a manager at this stage of my career.

Yes, I've been going so long that I was eligible to play in the World Seniors Championship! I wrote about the Legends event in Glenrothes and was pleased to see Joe Johnson, the 1986 world champion, pick up the baton and promote a proper World Championship for over-40s, which had TV coverage and fantastic crowds in Bradford. Jimmy White beat Steve Davis in the final. I lost my first match 2-0 to Nigel Bond, although the games were so short it was hard to judge my performance. I loved the weekend, though. It was great to see the old boys back together again and I would love to win the title because that would make me a world champion at junior, amateur, professional and senior level and it's hard to see anyone ever equalling that record.

I have opened a snooker club close to where I live, which will also serve as an academy to train new talent. Irish snooker needs some young stars to emerge. I'm still the Republic of Ireland's highest-ranked player and I'm in my forties. This is a chance for me to get involved and hopefully find some stars of the future. It's a new venture and new experience for me but with snooker starting to regain some of its lost popularity I think the time is right.

Away from snooker, Manchester United set a new record for winning the top flight the most times. Their win in the Premier League made it 19 to Liverpool's 18. This is down mainly to Sir Alex Ferguson's management of the club. He has been outstanding and my admiration for him grows with every year. The way the snooker circuit is going I probably won't have much time to go and see United in person from now on. In a way I hope I don't because it'll mean I'm still doing well in tournaments.

There's a buzz about snooker again and I still think I have a part to play. My enthusiasm for playing remains as strong as ever as I look to my future both inside and outside the game.

CHAPTER TWENTY-EIGHT

THE FUTURE

I hope my life and career have several more chapters to run. I still feel capable of competing at the top level and have no intention yet of hanging up my cue.

Snooker is in my blood. It's a huge, important part of my life and I want to continue playing on the circuit for as long as I can. I know there will come a time when that is no longer possible but I look at Steve Davis playing professionally well into his fifties and take inspiration from him. He still enjoys the game and gets results. I'm in my early forties now so I could have another decade or more of pro snooker ahead of me.

I'll hang on for as long as I can. You don't lose any dignity by carrying on even though you're no longer seriously contending for titles. Steve has done it, as has Jimmy White and if anything they are respected a lot more because it proves the appetite they still have after all their years on the tour. You can only admire that pure love for snooker and they certainly don't have anything to apologise for.

I love snooker and always will. Even though it has dealt me some huge disappointments, it has also been responsible for moments you couldn't buy. But every player faces the prospect of losing their best form and being unable to get it back, of not playing to the same high standard as you were once capable of. This happens in all sports and in snooker it can be a gradual decline or a sudden plummeting down the rankings. I've seen it happen to other successful players and it's frustrating when it ceases to be as enjoyable as it once was. I thought it was happening to me during the 2008/09 season but managed to haul myself out of that slump, which proved to be temporary rather than permanent.

I haven't given my future after my playing days a great deal of thought. I do love doing the media work, both for the BBC and for Irish TV and radio, and I'd like to continue with that. It would be a way of remaining connected with snooker. Other former champions have managed to keep their profiles high through the force of their personalities and that's good for snooker as well, because some of the older players, like Dennis Taylor, Willie Thorne and John Virgo, are good ambassadors for the sport. They keep snooker's profile high through their media appearances and could be used by the game much more than they are.

Quite a few of the younger players could learn a lot from some of the old timers. If you look at Terry Griffiths you see a former world champion widely respected and someone who can pass on so much wisdom to players coming through, which he does in his role as a coach. He's been there and done it, and having played snooker at the highest level, will be able to advise about tactics and coping with the often intense pressure. His love of the game is unwavering and I have a great respect for that.

I'd like to develop my media career but nothing beats playing or ever will. The buzz of going out in front of the crowd and performing is the reason we all play snooker. That's why Jimmy White is still so hungry. You can't beat putting on a show for the audience and them responding warmly towards you.

It will be difficult when the time comes to retire but I want to give something back to snooker. When I stop playing I might look at coaching or even management. I know that I will want to remain involved in some way.

I turned professional at a good time, when there was still plenty of money in the game and loads of tournaments to play in. There are signs that those times are returning, with more events and greater international development. It's hard to say where snooker is going to go in the future. It has had its boom time in the UK and Ireland and is unlikely to reach that level again but the world is our oyster and there's considerable evidence that global interest in the sport is higher than it has ever been.

They love it in China and Germany, where it will hopefully be sustained as a professional sport in the years to come. The Far East and Europe represent snooker's best chance of expansion.

We have to reach out to these places, where TV coverage has created millions of new fans, and not just rely on the traditional British market to keep the sport going. I hope to play some part in snooker's continuing story. It's had a remarkable history already and will hopefully enjoy a prosperous future.

As I think about my future I find myself reflecting on the past. When I look back I feel that above all I've been lucky. Lucky to have been born into a loving family. Lucky to have spent my life playing the game I love. Lucky to have travelled the world and experienced so many diverse and interesting cultures. Lucky to have met a variety of people from differing backgrounds. Lucky to have enjoyed the support of millions of people, most of whom I will never meet. Lucky to have met Sarah and been blessed with Christian. Lucky to have been able to appreciate it all and not take any of it for granted.

I'd have loved to have won more than I did. No matter how successful you've been, you always feel you could have done better, such is the nature of sport. A couple of finals went away from me and I have a few regrets, but who doesn't? When I started out I aspired to be a top player but I couldn't possibly know how my career would go or whether I would taste success at the highest level. My name will always be on that World Championship trophy and I'm assured of a place in snooker history. That's special to me – to be alongside all the great players forever. But it's not just about the record books: I have memories that I will cherish until my dying day, especially of coming back to Dublin the day after winning the title.

Everyone wants to be remembered. Snooker was my way of

making a mark on the world and I wouldn't change the decision I made as a teenager for anything. When I think back to when I was a young lad of 12 watching Alex Higgins winning the World Championship, it's unbelievable that I managed to emulate that. All those years in Jason's, in Ilford, slogging around the circuit, were worth it. I feel honoured to have played this sport for a living and to have hit the heights in the way I did.

Above all, I'm grateful to the game of snooker for the life it has given me.

KEN DOHERTY: CAREER RECORD

World ranking titles

1993 Welsh Open

1997 World Championship

2000 Malta Grand Prix

2001 Welsh Open

2001 Thailand Masters

2006 Malta Cup

Ranking finals: 17

Ranking semi-finals: 35

Ranking quarter-finals: 61

Other titles

1992 B&H Championship

1993, 1994, 1996 Pontins Professional Championship
1993, 1994 Scottish Masters
1996, 1998 European League
1997 Malta Grand Prix
2007 Pot Black
Highest competitive break: 145 (2004 Players Championship)

World Championship
Crucible appearances: 17
Finals: 3
Titles: 1
Semi-finals: 3
Quarter-finals: 8
Crucible centuries: 33
Highest break: 137 (1998)

Rankings
Seasons in top 16: 15
Seasons in top 8: 12
Seasons in top 4: 5
Highest ranking: 2 (2006/07)

All statistics correct as at end of 2010/11 season.